WORDS FROM THE
Stars

Similar titles from Random House Value Publishing, Inc.

14,000 Quips and Quotes

The Nasty Quote Book

WORDS FROM THE

Stars

Quips and Quotes from Mae West to the Backstreet Boys

☆ ☆ ☆ ☆ ☆ ☆ ☆ ☆

EDITED BY TREVOR HUNT

GRAMERCY BOOKS
NEW YORK

This 2001 edition is published by Gramercy Books™, an imprint of Random House Value Publishing, Inc. 280 Park Avenue, New York, N.Y. 10017.

Gramercy Books™ and design are trademarks of Random House Value Publishing, Inc.

Random House
New York • Toronto • London • Sydney • Auckland
http://www.randomhouse.com/

Interior design by Cathleen Bennett

Printed and bound in the United States of America

Library of Congress Cataloging-in-Publication Data

Words from the stars : quips and quotes from Mae West to the Backstreet Boys / edited by Trevor Hunt.
        p. cm.
    ISBN 0-517-21856-9
1. Motion picture actors and actresses–United States–Quotations. I. Hunt, Trevor.

PN1994.9 .W67 2001
791.43'028'092273–dc21

                                                        2001023836

987654321

Contents

☆ ☆ ☆ ☆ ☆ ☆ ☆ ☆

Contents

Gentlemen Prefer Blondes

or do they?

☆ ☆ ☆ ☆ ☆ ☆ ☆ ☆

If truth is beauty, how come no one has their hair done in a library?

–Lily Tomlin

I'm a ballbuster, blonde or brunette!

–Ashley Judd

I guess I look like a rock quarry that someone has dynamited.

–Charles Bronson

When I go to the beauty parlor, I always use the emergency entrance. Sometimes I go just for an estimate.

–Phyllis Diller

I wasn't fat, I was just Greek and Greeks are round, with big asses and big boobs.

–Jennifer Aniston

Hair has always been important.
—**Diana Ross**

God gave women intuition and femininity. And used proper-ly, that combination easily jumbles the brain of any men I've ever met.
—**Farrah Fawcett**

Never purchase beauty products in a hardware store.
—**Miss Piggy**

I'm not offended by all the dumb blonde jokes because I know I'm not dumb...and I also know I'm not blonde.
—**Dolly Parton**

I'm a big woman. I need big hair.
—**Aretha Franklin**

My fans want me with my hair.
—**Sarah Brightman**

I don't get acting jobs because of my looks.
—**Alec Baldwin**

Beauty, to me, is about being comfortable in your own skin. That, or a kick-ass red lipstick.
—**Gwyneth Paltrow**

I find it an effort to keep up appearances.
—**Dusty Springfield**

I like the way my own feet smell. I love to smell my sneakers when I take them off.

—Christina Ricci

Ava Gardner was the most beautiful woman in the world, and it's wonderful that she didn't cut up her face. She addressed aging by picking up her chin and receiving the light in a better way. And she looked like a woman. She never tried to look like a girl.

—Sharon Stone

I don't do much. I play an hour of tennis with a pro, five or six days a week. That's all I do. I worked out for years, but I got bored. I'm pretty careful about what I eat, but I'm not obsessed. I'm lucky genetically, I guess.

—Harrison Ford

How long can you be cute?

—Goldie Hawn

I can't bear being seen naked. I'm not exactly a tiny woman. When Sophia Loren is naked, this is a lot of nakedness.

—Sophia Loren

They tell me I'm about the only actor in town who doesn't at least know where his dress suit is.

—Clark Gable

It is better to be looked than overlooked.

—Mae West

I don't mind that I'm fat. You still get the same money

−Marlon Brando

It's a good thing that I was born a woman, or I'd have been a drag queen.

−Dolly Parton

I have a face like the behind of an elephant.

−Charles Laughton

I haven't got a cold. I talk like this all the time.

−June Allyson

People used to throw rocks at me because of my clothes. Now they wanna know where I buy them.

−Cyndi Lauper

A woman's dress should be like a barbed-wire fence: serving its purpose without obstructing the view.

−Sophia Loren

It's a huge change for your body. You don't even want to look in the mirror after you've had a baby, because your stomach is just hanging there like a Shar-Pei.

−Cindy Crawford

Being a celebrity is probably the closest to being a beautiful woman as you can get.

−Kevin Costner

Now my body is really womanly—a little too much so. It's something I can fall back on. When I don't know what else to do, I stick my chest out.

−Christina Ricci

I don't want to see pictures of Hollywood stars in their dressing gowns taking out the rubbish. It ruins the fantasy.

−Sarah Brightman

I dress for women, and undress for men.

−Angie Dickinson

I have a little bit of a belly, a tiny bit of pooch. It's the one thing I don't want to lose. I just like having some softness.

−Nicole Kidman

No one ever told me I was pretty when I was a little girl. All little girls should be told they are pretty, even if they aren't.

−Marilyn Monroe

I'm the female equivalent of a counterfeit twenty-dollar bill. Half of what you see is a pretty good reproduction, and the rest is a fraud.

−Cher

I think your whole life shows in your face and you should be proud of that.

−Lauren Bacall

Growing up, I was the plain one. I had no style. I was the tough kid with the comb in the back pocket and feathered hair.

−Cameron Diaz

Just standing around looking beautiful is so boring, really boring, so boring.

−Michelle Pfeiffer

I owe a lot of my performance to the corset I had to wear....The blood rushes to your face when you wear those things. So that explains "radiant."

−Emma Thompson

I think onstage nudity is disgusting, shameful, and damaging to all things American. But if I were twenty-two with a great body, it would be artistic, tasteful, patriotic, and a progressive religious experience.

−Shelley Winters

On my best [day], I am a seven-point-seven. I could be a hard eight if I felt great. If I went on a good run and had on my best pair of jeans, I could feel right on the money.

−Julia Roberts

I'm not handsome in the classical sense. The eyes droop, the mouth is crooked, the teeth aren't straight, the voice sounds like a *mafioso* pallbearer.

−Sylvester Stallone

My breasts are beautiful, and I gotta tell you, they've gotten a lot of attention for what is relatively short screen time.

–**Jamie Lee Curtis**

Retirement must be wonderful. I mean, you can suck in your stomach for only so long.

–**Burt Reynolds**

When you're not thin and blonde, you come up with a personality real quick.

–**Kathy Najimy**

Just call me a nice, clean-cut Mongolian boy.

–**Yul Brynner**

My look is attainable. Women can look like Audrey Hepburn by flipping out their hair, buying the large sunglasses, and the little sleeveless dresses.

–**Audrey Hepburn**

...I hate to make publicity stills or to have my picture taken...I put it off just as long as I can possibly get away with it, then I finally go and act like a ham standing before a camera in riding boots or clutching a pipe between my teeth.

–**Clark Gable**

With that big cellulite ass rolling across the screen, it had to be me. I don't know where you'd find buttocks like mine, dear.

–**Tracey Ullman**

For most people, tucking is a nonevent. But for those of us who tend to the round, it isn't so simple. To tuck or not to tuck? That is the question. It comes loaded with issues of self-perception and self-acceptance.

—**Rosie O'Donnell**

I don't think I'm too thin at all. I understand when people say, "Well your face gets gaunt," but to get your bottom half to be the right size, your face might have to be a little gaunt. You choose your battles.

—**Courteney Cox**

I was so skinny, they gave me the nickname *stechetto*—the stick. I was tall, thin, ugly, and dark like an Arab girl. I looked strange. All eyes. No flesh on my bones.

—**Sophia Loren**

I feel more naked with makeup on than I do without it.

—**Brooke Shields**

People have been so busy relating to how I look, it's a miracle I didn't become a self-conscious blob of protoplasm.

—**Robert Redford**

I've actually gone to the zoo and had monkeys shout to me from their cages, "I'm in here when you're walking around like that?"

—**Robin Williams on his hairiness**

I'm too tall to be a girl. I'm between a chick and a broad.

—**Julia Roberts**

I may be a dumb blonde, but I'm not that blonde.
—Patricia Neal

In high school, I dressed up as every James Bond girl. I was a teenage Pussy Galore.
—Winona Ryder

I never go out unless I look like Joan Crawford the movie star. If you want to see the girl next door, go next door.
—Joan Crawford

Look your best—who said love is blind?
—Mae West

All I can say is if they show my butt in a movie, it better be a wide shot.
—Jennifer Lopez

I would rather lose a good earring than be caught without make-up.
—Lana Turner

I never thought I'd land in pictures with a face like mine.
—Audrey Hepburn

I don't have false teeth. Do you think I'd buy teeth like these?
—Carol Burnett

I have these big piano-playing hands. I feel like I should be picking potatoes.
—Sandra Bullock

I had huge zits...a huge cold sore on my lip...stretch marks all over my butt...birthmarks, bruises. You name it, it's airbrushed.

—Jenny McCarthy

I've got all this pressure to keep trim as Sporty Spice—I used to drink lager and blackcurrant, but I had to stop because I was getting a beer gut. I could have ended up being Fat Old Lazy Spice.

—Mel C, "Spice Girl"

I like to dress sexy, but not in a really obvious way. Sexy in a kind of virginal way.

—Posh Spice

If you haven't cried, your eyes can't be beautiful.

—Sophia Loren

I'm much more than a pair of breasts. I represent success, hard work, and fun.

—Pamela Anderson

The only gal who came near to me in the sex appeal department was pretty little Marilyn Monroe. All the others had were big boobs.

—Mae West

It [being handsome] can open doors. When I think about those who don't get the opportunity...I wrestle with that a bit.

—Brad Pitt

My mother told me that actresses are very pretty with big eyes. She said I was not pretty. It would be more suitable for me to become a primary or nursery teacher. I did not think I would be an actress.

−Gong Li, China's most famous actress

Before I was even in high school, I had dark circles under my eyes. Rumor was that I was a junkie. I have dark circles under my eyes, deal with it.

−Benicio Del Toro

I don't want to be known as the Aerosmith chick, but it's fun to put on the boots and makeup and act like a tough girl.

−Alicia Silverstone

Tall, sandy blonde, with sort of blue eyes, skinny in places, fat in others. An average gal.

−Uma Thurman

I wasn't a cheerleader or the prom queen. I don't move through the world with a mirror in front of my face, and I've never been attracted to projects that had an emphasis on what I look like.

−Michael Michele

If God wanted us to be naked, why did he invent sexy lingerie?

−Shannen Doherty

You can wear red with red hair. They say you can't, but I can, and I do−and I look great.

−Molly Ringwald

My appearance is of minimal interest to me.

—Josh Hartnett

I was teased because I had a really flat-looking nose and before I got braces my teeth used to stick out a bit.

—Catherine Zeta-Jones

I can make a scene that's not supposed to be sexy, very sexy. It's a power you're born with. It's not a physical thing, it comes from inside. It's all in the eyes.

—Tara Reid

If you're not feeling good about you, what you're wearing outside doesn't mean a thing.

—Leontyne Price

I think any girl who comes to Hollywood with sex symbol or bombshell hanging over her has a rough road.

—Kim Basinger

What I find interesting is that I am the largest woman who's ever been on the cover of *Vogue*. Also, they just don't have black women on the cover, not to mention women over 30. That's why it was so phenomenal.

—Oprah Winfrey

I squint because I can't take too much light.

—Clint Eastwood

I used to go around looking as frumpy as possible because it was inconceivable you could be attractive as well as be smart. It wasn't until I started being myself, the way I like to turn out to meet people, that I started to get any work.

—**Catherine Zeta-Jones**

My best feature's my smile. And smiles—pray heaven—don't get fat.

—**Jack Nicholson**

Taking joy in life is a woman's best cosmetic.

—**Rosalind Russell**

Heartthrobs are a dime a dozen.

—**Brad Pitt**

There's no way I set out to be a certain kind of symbol—the way I dress is the way I am, the way I live my life.

—**Pamela Anderson**

I do a forty-minute pool workout every morning, and I have an exercycle. When you're eighteen, you don't have to work out. As an actor, I realized I had to keep my body in shape.

—**Charlton Heston**

It matters more what's in a woman's face than what's on it.

—**Claudette Colbert**

I've considered having my nose fixed. But I didn't trust anyone enough. If I could do it myself with a mirror...

— **Barbra Streisand**

The real American type can never be a ballet dancer. The legs are too long, the body too supple and the spirit too free for this school of affected grace and toe walking.

— **Isadora Duncan**

When I look at myself, I am so beautiful, I scream with joy.

— **Maria Montez**

I have a gym in the house. I run some mornings and take a sauna. But I don't work on my arm and then go to the mirror and see if it grew. I'm not that type of guy. And I'm not into fashion at all either.

— **Antonio Banderas**

I think I know my weight by years. I can probably tell you what I weighed almost every year since I started in this business. When I first came to Chicago, nobody had ever seen anybody like me on television before. I was 238 pounds—this overweight, dark-skinned black woman. I remember I was interviewing some models one day, and these size-two women were talking about their weight problems. I was like, "Get over it!"

— **Oprah Winfrey**

I'm magnificent. I'm five feet eleven inches and I weigh one hundred thirty-five pounds, and I look like a racehorse.

— **Julie Newmar**

Most nights I end up wearing a wife beater T-shirt and boxers.

—**Jessica Alba**

God made a very obvious choice when he made me voluptuous; why would I go against what he decided for me? My limbs work, so I'm not going to complain about the way my body is shaped.

—**Drew Barrymore**

I'm more of a jeans and T-shirt kind of girl.

—**Tara Reid**

I like women to look like women. I hated grunge. No one's more feminist than me, but you don't have to look as if you don't give a—you know.

—**Catherine Zeta-Jones**

I'm basically a sexless geek. Look at me, I have pasty-white skin, I have acne scars and I'm five-foot-nothing. Does that sound like a real sexual dynamo to you?

—**Mike Myers**

W called me "the young Delta Burke." It's so silly. I weigh 105 pounds and wear a size two, but for some reason I'm a heavyweight.

—**Christina Ricci**

I felt guilty when I lost 30 lbs. to get a part, because I don't like the way Hollywood works—they usually prefer actresses who are half-starved. Because of our screwed-up society, the biggest deterrent to a woman in Hollywood is fat. And then, after losing all that weight, I didn't even get the role! I put the weight back on in a minute or so, and now I feel better.

—Janeane Garofalo

I'm just naturally slender. My mom is small, too. Sometimes, I actually have to eat a lot, or I'll get too skinny, and then I look real yucky.

—Nikki Cox

I've got a broken nose. Freckles. I have broken capillaries around my eyes, and my neck's funny from an operation.

—Catherine Zeta-Jones

I see my face in the mirror and go, "I'm a Halloween costume? That's what they think of me?"

—Drew Carey

I freaked after *Dangerous Liaisons* when I was being described as, you know, a vivacious beauty. I was pretty uncomfortable with that. I didn't see myself as a sexual creature.

—Uma Thurman

I feel sexy when I get out of the tub—your skin is fresh and you've put up your hair without looking.

—Shania Twain

I'm a lot tougher than I look. I may be five-two, but I…am…tough.

—Reese Witherspoon

I wouldn't do nudity in films. To act with my clothes on is a performance; to act with my clothes off is a documentary.

—Julia Roberts

I thought they would give [the Tony Soprano role] role to someone who's a little more suave, a little more like these dons are usually. I'm not like that at all.

—James Gandolfini

I had been told time and again..."You're not pretty enough to be an ingenue. You don't have the style of a leading lady. You'll have to wait until you're old enough to play character parts. That's when you'll come into your own.

—Vivian Vance

Normally those girls wouldn't have given me a second look if I hadn't been such a hit in the school shows...most of those girls were head and shoulders taller than me. But it made me popular and I could get almost anyone I wanted to come to the school dances with me. Some of them thought I was bloody marvelous and pretty soon I began to believe them.

—Gene Kelly

I don't think I am esthetically beautiful. I am just photogenic.

—Catherine Zeta-Jones

I don't need plastic in my body to validate me as a woman.

—Courtney Love

You never see a man walking down the street with a woman who has a little potbelly and a bald spot.

–Elayne Boosler

I have flabby thighs, but fortunately my stomach covers them.

–Joan Rivers

Kiss my shapely big fat ass.

–K.T. Oslin

The Sweet Smell of Success

☆ ☆ ☆ ☆ ☆ ☆ ☆ ☆

I don't know anything about music. In my line you don't have to.

–Elvis Presley

There's a huge loss of privacy, but there's a huge trade-off, too. I can get baseball tickets anytime I want.

–Tom Hanks

I'm ambitious. But if I weren't as talented as I am ambitious, I would be a gross monstrosity

–Madonna

In 1975 I became big and it took me until 1985 to learn how to deal with it.

–John Travolta

I never think of myself as an icon. What is in other people's minds is not in my mind. I just do my thing.

–Audrey Hepburn

I don't have to be well-informed. I'm well endowed. I'm a star.

–Bette Midler

People ask me how far I've come. And I tell them 12 feet. From the audience to the stage!

–David Lee Roth

I never wanted to be famous. I only wanted to be great.

–Ray Charles

The toughest thing about being a success is that you've got to keep on being a success.

–Irving Berlin

I've outdone anyone you can name–Mozart, Beethoven, Bach, Strauss, Irving Berlin–he wrote 1,001 tunes. I wrote 5,500.

–James Brown

I was the kind nobody thought could make it. I had a funny Boston accent. I couldn't pronounce my R's. I wasn't a beauty.

–Barbara Walters

Being a sex symbol was rather like being a convict.

–Raquel Welch

I always felt I'd make it. There were some moments of doubt, but I knew something would eventually happen. When [my aunt] Mimi used to throw away things I'd written or drawn, I used to say, "You'll regret that when I'm famous," and I meant it.

–John Lennon

I think my fans will follow me into our combined old age. Real musicians and real fans stay together for a long, long time.

—Bonnie Raitt

I'm the lady next door when I'm not on stage.

—Aretha Franklin

Sometimes I wish I weren't famous.

—Tammy Wynette

Success always necessitates a degree of ruthlessness. Given the choice of friendship or success, I'd probably choose success.

—Sting

I think people like me best when I just peel back the layers and speak about what's there. I think that's when people are affected by my music the most.

—Melissa Etheridge

It turns out there is no "destination." There's no point of saying, "Okay, I got a movie—my *Good Will* thing—so, it's okay. I can relax." Because for three years, that's all I did—I was trying to get that movie made. That doesn't really happen. What happens is a kind of restlessness and anxiety. So, I keep busy. What's more satisfying is the struggle rather than sitting back and relishing achievement

—Ben Affleck

I am where I am by the grace of God, but I haven't had to do anything [other than] just work hard to get where I am.

—Denzel Washington

At first all I wanted to be was famous; then I realized that fame had nothing to do with talent. I felt that I didn't do anything quite well enough, that I was one of those people who was famous but not very talented. So I said, okay, I'll be the Dinah Shore of the Seventies, on TV all the time but nobody quite knows why.

−Cher

That's the way it is with Cher. She's very demanding of the men in her life. She expected me to lead the way to success....

−Sonny Bono

My career should adapt to me. Fame is like a VIP pass to wherever you want to go.

−Leonardo DiCaprio

It's hard for a man to live with a successful woman—they seem to resent you so much. Very few men are generous enough to accept success in their women.

−Shirley Bassey

I think success is not a reason to quit.

−Kenny Rogers

You can be up to your boobies in white satin, with gardenias in your hair and no sugar cane for miles, but you can still be working on a plantation.

−Billie Holiday

For someone who had been in the shadow of his father for all those years, to be acknowledged by my peers and get even the [Oscar] nomination—it meant a tremendous amount. For those of us who are second-generation, there is a question of: No matter how hard you've worked and tried, do you really deserve it?

– Michael Douglas

It's marvelous to be popular, but foolish to think it will last.

– Dusty Springfield

It's a little depressing to become number one because the only place you can go from there is down.

– Doris Day

It's a marvelous feeling when someone says, "I want to do this song of yours" because they've connected to it. That's what I'm after.

– Mary Chapin-Carpenter

It's all happening so fast, I've got to put the brakes on or I'll smack into something.

– Mel Gibson

My daddy told me if I was gonna quit school that I would have to be damn sure that I was gonna really work hard at music, because I wouldn't be able to do anything else—which was fine with me because I didn't want to do anything else.

– Mark Chestnutt

I like to keep growing. I haven't gotten anywhere, as far as I'm concerned.

– Benicio Del Toro

People want you to be crazy, an out-of-control teen brat. They want you miserable, just like them. They don't want heroes; what they want is to see you fall.

−Leonardo DiCaprio

I'm like a chameleon in that I take on the colors of success or failure, happy or sad, depending on what's going on, or how it seems to be going.

−Mary Tyler Moore

The truth is, I've made about 30 movies in 30 years, and I've been criticized for 30 years for not making more movies.

−Dustin Hoffman

I'm not Jacko, I'm Jackson... "Wacko Jacko"—where did that come from? Some English tabloid. I have a heart and I have feelings. I feel that when you do that to me, it's not nice.

−Michael Jackson

Success has gone to my hips.

−Dolly Parton

I never thought in terms of any kind of fame. There's no way you can prepare for that.

−Brad Pitt

Don't you love this face?
I'll autograph my pictures
I brought some just in case
"Hey that's MY guitar!"−"that's her guitar"

I can't help bein' a star—
shoop shoop shoop-be-doop-be-doop
With all this talent I'll go far
I can't help bein' a star

—Miss Piggy

I'm an instant star, just add water and stir.

—David Bowie

I don't feel like a legend. I feel like a work in progress.

—Barbra Streisand

I couldn't wait for success, so I went ahead without it.

—Jonathan Winters

I like writing songs. I like the camaraderie and I like touring.
I love playing bass. And then there's free beer.

—Keanu Reeves

Success is like death. The more successful you become,
the higher the houses in the hills get and the higher the
fences get.

—Kevin Spacey

Ain't nowhere else in the world [but America] where you can go
from driving a truck to driving a Cadillac overnight. Nowhere.

—Elvis Presley

Hollywood's a place where they'll pay you a thousand dollars
for a kiss, and fifty cents for your soul.

—Marilyn Monroe

I almost wish I could be more exciting, that I could match what is happening out there to me.
— **Whitney Houston**

What I do, I do the best. Maybe I'm not as versatile as other actors, but for the type of thing I do, I do it well.
— **Clint Eastwood**

It was all so amazing. The excessiveness of it all. The weird thing is I thought *Saturday Night Fever* was just going to be a stepping stone. We did the movie thinking it would be a small art film.
— **John Travolta**

Success is like reaching an important birthday and finding you're exactly the same.
— **Audrey Hepburn**

The image we have would be impossible for Mickey Mouse to maintain. We're just ... normal people.
— **Karen Carpenter**

I'm not a superstar. Jim Carrey makes $20 million a movie. I make a weird face when they tell me I have to pay $8.50 to see one.
— **Chris Rock**

It isn't what they say about you, it's what they whisper.
— **Errol Flynn**

Celebrity is death...celebrity—that's the worst thing that can happen to an actor.
— **John Cusack**

I walk down the street, and I'm treated like an ordinary black guy, which runs the gamut from cops looking weird at me, to women clutching their purses, to just regular looks. Then they realize who I am and they're all nice and smiley.

– Jesse L. Martin

There's a point where I think that if you don't maintain a certain kind of humility and graciousness, and be incredibly supportive and nonconfrontational, then I think the press and people enjoy your popularity. But when you start to become a little difficult and controversial, and combative, and I think a little too verbal in your criticism or too opinionated, then the pendulum swings the other way. So you know what? It's okay that you're an actor. But like, be grateful, all right?

– Sylvester Stallone

For an actress to be a success, she must have the face of a Venus, the brains of a Minerva, the grace of Terpsichore, the memory of a Macaulay, the figure of Juno, and the hide of a rhinoceros.

– Ethel Barrymore

Don't say Aretha is making a comeback, because I've never been away!

– Aretha Franklin

Success is a double-edged sword, and always will be because when you enjoy it, you enjoy it with an understanding of what it's worth and what it's for, and that's for self-happiness.

– David Boreanaz

I'm the most misunderstood, misquoted person I know, honestly.

—Dusty Springfield

I'd love to be a pop idol. Of course, my groupies are now between [the ages of] 40 and 50.

—Kevin Bacon

I don't know why it [stardom] happened—but it's kinda nice. Maybe it's because I'm someone off the streets. Maybe people related to me.

—Steve McQueen

I'm sort of a gay success story, a very inspirational one. What happened to me is exactly the opposite of what closeted people fear: They think they'll lose everything if they come out. This did not happen to me at all.

—Melissa Etheridge

It's very little trouble for me to accommodate [my fans], unless I'm actually taking a pee at the time.

—Harrison Ford

The only reason they come to see me is that I know life is great—and they know I know it.

—Clark Gable

The only thing I can control is my work. I can control how I dance, how I act in a movie...If you start worrying about what's being said about you, you'll go crazy.

—Jennifer Lopez

I am terribly shy, but of course no one believes me. Come to think of it, neither would I.

–**Carol Channing**

Being a performer was always my destiny. When I was born, the doctors didn't have to pop me to get me going. It was like, "Thank you, thank you. I am here!" I was ready to party.

–**Whoopi Goldberg**

Knowing what you can not do is more important than knowing what you can do. In fact, that's good taste.

–**Lucille Ball**

I'm just like anyone. I cut and I bleed. And I embarrass easily.

–**Michael Jackson**

The average celebrity meets, in one year, ten times the amount of people that the average person meets in his entire life.

–**Jack Nicholson**

I first saw the "star" thing in my son. He'd see people coming up to me, paying attention or asking for autographs and he'd ask me, "How come people ask you to sign papers?" I said: "Well, they see me in the theatres and it's sort of a custom that some jerk invented years ago."

–**Clint Eastwood**

A man is a success if he gets up in the morning and gets to bed at night, and in between he does what he wants to do.

–**Bob Dylan**

Celebrity is a pretty stunning thing. At first I was like, "They love me! Oh, I love them, too." And suddenly, I was tap-dancing on my pedestal and it was whack! Face down in the dirt.

—Sharon Stone

What's been deeply moving to me is that there have been two or three times in my life where people have confessed to me that their lives have changed because of a film that I've been in...That moves me. That excites me. The whole fan thing, people coming up to me and saying, hey you're great...Thank you, but that doesn't resonate for me.

—Alan Arkin

In the final analysis, it's true that fame is unimportant. No matter how great a man is, the size of his funeral usually depends on the weather.

—Rosemary Clooney

Models are like baseball players. We make a lot of money quickly, but all of a sudden we're 30 years old, we don't have a college education, we're qualified for nothing, and we're used to a very nice lifestyle. The best thing is to marry a movie star.

—Cindy Crawford

Celebrity was a long time in coming; it will go away. Everything goes away.

—Carol Burnett

A lapse in public taste led me to become a leading man and I take advantage of that opportunity. I'm like a fireman. When I go out on call, I want to put out a big fire, I don't want to put out a fire in a dumpster. Not some trash fire.

—**Harrison Ford**

As soon as you find the key to success, somebody always changes the lock.

—**Tracey Ullman**

I kinda see my current position like this: "Here's your five minutes in the toy store, so you gotta do all the good movies you can before Chuck Woolery rings the bell."

—**Ben Affleck**

There are, I think, three countries left in the world where I can go and I'm not as well-known as I am here. I'm a pretty big star, folks—I don't have to tell you. Superstar, I guess you could say.

—**Bruce Willis**

Lots of people want to ride with you in the limo, but what you want is someone who will take the bus with you when the limo breaks down.

—**Oprah Winfrey**

It's kinda nice to be remembered by your peers and your fans, because you can achieve a lot of success and be a creep too! But we try to be nice, just normal people.

—**Karen Carpenter**

Better to be king for a night than a schmuck for a lifetime.

–**Robert De Niro**

I had this frightening experience at the *Grease* opening in London when I thought the roof of the car was going to cave in under the crush. I genuinely thought my life was about to end. It was panic point for me. And yet it was exciting too. Part of me was loving it.

–**John Travolta**

I don't enjoy public performances and being up on a stage. I don't enjoy the glamour. Like tonight, I am up on stage and my feet hurt.

–**Barbra Streisand**

We're celebrities, actors, actresses, monkeys, clowns. Now all I want to do is maybe amuse people.

–**Uma Thurman**

People hate me because I am a multi-faceted, talented, wealthy, internationally famous genius.

–**Jerry Lewis**

My mother drew a distinction between achievement and success. She said that achievement is the knowledge that you have studied and worked hard and done the best that is in you. Success is being praised by others, and that's nice too, but not as important or satisfying. Always aim for achievement and forget about success.

–**Helen Hayes**

Many a man owes his success to his first wife, and his second wife to his success.
— **Jim Backus**

The worst part of success is to try to find someone who is happy for you.
— **Bette Midler**

I don't feel like I imagine an idol is supposed to feel.
— **Paul McCartney**

If I am a legend, then why am I so lonely?
— **Judy Garland**

A career is born in public—talent in privacy.
— **Marilyn Monroe**

Bad press put me where I am. If they didn't write about me at all, I wouldn't be famous.
— **Delta Burke**

There are five stages to an actor's career. First, "Who's Robby Benson?" Then, "Get me Robby Benson." "Get me a Robby Benson type," that's three. "Get me a young Robby Benson," four. And five? "Who's Robby Benson?"
— **Robby Benson**

If I hadn't made it as an actor, I might have wound up a hood.
— **Steve McQueen**

My career is going better now than when I was younger. It used to be that I'd get the girl but not the part. Now I get the part but not the girl.

–Michael Caine

Success for me is having ten honeydew melons and eating only the top half of each one.

–Barbra Streisand

We've become so glorified in the movie-star system that it's become this artificial royalty. The truth is that we're circus clowns.

–Nicholas Cage

The biggest gift your fans can give you is just treating you like a human being. If the price of fame is that you have to be isolated form the people you write for, then that's too high a price to pay.

–Bruce Springsteen

I don't know the key to success, but the key to failure is trying to please everybody.

–Bill Cosby

Death will be a great relief. No more interviews.

–Katharine Hepburn

A lot of fellows nowadays have a B.A., M.D., or Ph.D. Unfortunately, they don't have a J.O.B.

–Fats Domino

Always be smarter than the people who hire you.

—Lena Horne

A celebrity is a person who works hard all his life to become well known, and then wears dark glasses to avoid being recognized.

—Fred Allen

If all four of us had to stand up in front of a million fans and they had to line up behind the one they liked best, I think Paul would get most, John and George would be joint second, and Ringo would be last.

—Ringo Starr

I got a bit bored with acting and very much bored of being on the celebrity carousel. That's why I think I've appeared in just one film in the past three and a half years, which is disgraceful, really. But they've been the most enjoyable three and a half years of my life.

—Hugh Grant

If anybody wanted to photograph my life, they'd get bored in a day. "Here's Matt at home learning his lines. Here's Matt researching in aisle six of his local library." A few hours of that and they'd go home.

—Matt Damon

I am the King of All Media.

—Howard Stern

If your record doesn't sell that well, man, who cares? All the satisfaction I need... comes when I step out onstage and see the people. That's awesome. I love that.

−**Harry Connick Jr.**

I know I've been lucky in an awful lot of ways. But I think the luckiest thing that ever happened to me is that I'm already beginning to realize my greatest ambition....All my life, I've wanted to be an actor, though I never was in any school plays or recited a line other than the Gettysburg Address for my 6th grade homeroom class. But always sticking in the back of my head was the idea that somehow, someday, I'd like to get the chance to act.

−**Elvis Presley**

Once in one's life, for one mortal moment, one must make a grab for immortality; if not, one has not lived.

−**Sylvester Stallone**

It started in second grade. I was in music class and we were practicing for the Christmas assembly. One day I started fooling around by mocking the musicians on a record. The teacher thought she'd embarrass me by making me get up and do what was doing in front of the whole class. So I went up and did it. She laughed, and the whole class went nuts. My teacher asked me to do my routine for the Christmas assembly, and I did. That was the beginning of the end.

−**Jim Carrey**

Now, I'm not the first person you think of after Al Pacino, but luckily we have the same agent.

–Kevin Spacey

I don't like the glamorous nights so much. I usually leave depressed and I don't know why. Maybe it's the forced politeness. I like the local bar with money in the jukebox and a pretty girl next to me.

–Vince Vaughn

I'm not a diva. I'm a tadpole trying to be a frog.

–Toni Braxton

When my enemies stop hissing, I shall know I'm slipping.

–Maria Callas

Sometimes, today, I stand with Russell Downing, the manager of the finest, largest cinema in the world, the Radio City Music Hall in New York, in a quiet darkened corner, and listen to that huge audience roaring with laughter at something I've done, the tilt of my head or a facial reaction, and joy seems to burst within me.

–Cary Grant

I don't want to be a personality.

–Richard Gere

I love the work itself, and I love to be working. It's the peripheral stuff that really tires you out, stuff I never expected to encounter in this business. It's the photo shoots, the frickin' Leno interviews. It's those kinds of things that just drain you.

–Michelle Williams

I'm like old shoes. I've never been hip. I think the reason I'm still here is that I was never enough in fashion that I had to be replaced by something new.

–**Harrison Ford**

What counts to the artist is performance, not publicity. Guys who don't know me, already they've typed me as an oddball.

–**James Dean**

The first time I met her [Princess Diana] was after months of really microscopic attention on me, and she said, "How are you dealing with the attention?" and I said "Well, not very well". She said "It never gets better". Ironically enough, it never did for her, but it's different for me.

–**Catherine Zeta-Jones**

I don't really go to the spots where the paparazzi and the autograph seekers go, so I see them very rarely and I can deal with it. If I lived here [in Los Angeles] and I went to a lot of Hollywood parties and all that kind of stuff, I'd probably go nuts, but I don't do that. So unless people decide to follow me back to Minnesota... I feel pretty much like I'm in a good spot.

–**Josh Hartnett**

I don't want to know what my persona in Hollywood is. I don't want to start believing what all the other people's hype is.

–**Natasha Henstridge**

One of the steps you take to become a star: Learn to speak American.

−**Goran Visnjic**

That's the trouble with being me. At this point, nobody gives a damn what my problem is. I could literally have a tumor on the side of my head and they'd be like, "'Yeah, big deal. I'd eat a tumor every morning for the kinda money you're pulling down."

−**Jim Carrey**

I was a teen star. That's disgusting enough.

−**John Cusack**

We walked around casinos, and everyone was always looking at Kevin. I almost never got recognized because I looked like Tonya Harding. [on her bleached-blonde hair while filming *Pay It Forward*

−**Helen Hunt**

I certainly hope I'm not still answering child-star questions by the time I reach menopause.

−**Christina Ricci**

I suppose I sometimes used to act like I wasn't a human being... Sometimes I look back at myself and remember things I used to say, or my hairstyle, and I cringe.

−**Madonna**

Being a celebrity is probably the closest to being a beautiful woman as you can get.

−**Kevin Costner**

This huge life-changing moment of going from zero to ninety in two seconds!

−**Catherine Bell**

I like writing songs. I like the camaraderie of the band. I like touring. I love playing bass. And then there's free beer.

−**Keanu Reeves on being a rock star**

I'm not that ambitious any more. I just like my privacy. I wish I really wasn't talked about at all.

−**Barbra Streisand**

Reporters ask me what I feel China should do about Tibet. Who cares what I think China should do? I'm a f---ing actor. I'm here for entertainment, basically, when you whittle everything away. I'm a grown man who puts on makeup.

−**Brad Pitt**

In my early days I was a sepia Hedy Lamarr. Now I'm black and a woman, singing my own way.

−**Lena Horne**

Can I handle [fame] now? As opposed to not having handled it before? ... Just a little bit "maybe."... When it first comes upon you, it's like being hit with a big tsunami in the ocean and you panic and then you realize, "If I just calm down and see which way the bubbles are going, everything will be OK." So I'd have to say yes. Like anything, the more you do it, the more relaxed you become with it.

−**Julia Roberts**

Failure is inevitable. Success is elusive.

−Steven Spielberg

I never actually expected success, but it doesn't surprise me when it comes because I know how much work I put into what I do.

−Russell Crowe

My definition of success is control.

−Kenneth Branagh

No one ever did anything for me. I don't owe anything to anyone.

−James Dean

I didn't expect that I would feel the way I did after receiving an Oscar. As I said, it's not about deserving it. It just was sort of my turn. It's my turn. The feeling afterwards is hard to describe. Because you go around and you live and people are aware you won an Oscar. And they come up to you and congratulate you. Which keeps it afloat. That went on for a couple of weeks. I've never experienced that. It was like winning something at the Olympics.

−Al Pacino

You have to brush your teeth. I'm no longer on the fence about that one.

−Giovanni Ribisi

I hear from people who watch [*MASH*] six and seven times a day. It scares me.

−Alan Alda

[Fame] has complicated my life a little, but not enormously. I had to learn to be a public person, but fame has given me a good deal of control over my career, which I otherwise would not have had. Also, chances to work with some extraordinary men and women.

–Charlton Heston

To follow without halt, one aim; there is the secret of success. And success? What is it? I do not find it in the applause of the theater. It lies rather in the satisfaction of accomplishment.

–Anna Pavlova

It's been quite a roller-coaster ride...In this business, it's often all about hype, record sales, and a crazy schedule of traveling, performances, and it can be easy to get lost in all that. But for me, the greatest thing is being able to interact with fans and touch people's lives. I know that's a greater accomplishment than selling records. For that I give thanks. I simply love the job I'm doing.

–Christine Aguilera

I've about had it—the agencies, the winking, the networks, the ratings. Anyone who thinks TV is an art medium is crazy—it's an advertising medium.

–Robert Altman

Charlie Brown is the one person I identify with. C.B. is such a loser. He wasn't even the star of his own Halloween special.

–Chris Rock

Laurence Olivier: "Make up your mind, dear heart. Do you want to be a great actor or a household word?"
Richard Burton: "Both."

The first eight years of schooling was with all white people. So that helped me to understand how white people think. I think that transition is what helped me bridge the gap, because that's what my success has really been about: bridging the gap between the black community and the white community.

−Will Smith

Don't aim for success if you want it; just do what you love and believe in, and it will come naturally.

−David Frost

The press portrayed me as a kind of post-World War II version of Martha Stewart−"the Mermaid Tycoon," as I was dubbed on the cover of *Life*; the perfect homemaker; the Hollywood glamour queen; and a sex symbol in a bathing suit−all rolled into one....The world remembers me as a movie star, but most of my life I have thought about myself in various family roles− as daughter, sister, wife, and, above all, mother.

−Esther Williams

Success? You can't get a big head about it. When people stare at me, they could be whispering to their friend, "That guy sucks! Have you seen him before? He's horrible."

−David Spade

Whenever you step outside, you're on, brother, you're on.

−Sammy Davis, Jr.

You're only as good as your last picture.

−Marie Dressler

I want a sandwich named after me.

—Jon Stewart

If you can't make a career out of two DeMille films, you shouldn't be in this business.

—Charlton Heston

I wanted *Raging Bull*. I wanted *Casino*. I got *Rocky and Bullwinkle*. But that's OK, because I still get to tell people I've worked with Robert DeNiro.

—Rene Russo

We are not that flash, me or the missus [Madonna]. In fact, we are quite low-maintenance.

—Guy Ritchie

My movies were the kind they show in prisons and airplanes, because nobody can leave.

—Burt Reynolds

I honestly do not think about celebrity or image or sexual expectations on me. It only comes up when people have a list of questions. But what I am told is that there is a quality that I have onscreen, where it's a little bit of everything

—Richard Gere

It'd be stupid for me to sit here and say that there aren't kids who look up to me, but my responsibility is not to them. I'm not a baby sitter.

—Eminem

I get to stay at a nice hotel while I film and they're paying me well and it's a nice big part. *That's* why I do it. All the rest actors talk about is horseshit.

—Anthony Hopkins

In two years' time I want to be able to take my son to the park and not have to explain why 20 people with cameras are running after us.

—Catherine Zeta-Jones

I'm not the Beatles. I'm me. Paul isn't the Beatles...The Beatles are the Beatles. Separately, they are separate.

—John Lennon

You have only a short period of time in your life to make your mark, and I'm there now.

—George Clooney

I was told to avoid the business all together because of the rejection. People would say to me, "Don't you want to have a normal job and a normal family?" I guess that would be good advice for some people, but I wanted to act.

—Jennifer Aniston

On a good night, I get underwear, bras, and hotel-room keys thrown onstage... You start to think that you're Tom Jones.

—Keanu Reeves

I'm a movie star. Can I talk to my entertainment lawyer?

—Natasha Lyonne on arrest for drunken driving

Every place that you show up, someone is going to recognize you, but people are still polite and proud of what you're doing. So it's, like, sort of OK. It's not like you feel attacked or something.

—Goran Visnjic

[The hype] just doesn't help me at all, so I've just got to stay away from it.

—Josh Hartnett

... I just had a lot of faith [I'd make it to the top]. I had a vision so strong that I would just be up at night just thinking how to be different from other comedians. I used to watch the mannerisms of Richard Pryor and Eddie Murphy. I would say, "I have to combine all that with something else to really be a good comedian." I just dreamed and dreamed and it came true. And I'm still dreaming, I got a lot of stuff left.

—Chris Tucker

I was walking down Madison Avenue, saw a beautiful tie in the window, and walked into the haberdashery. The guy was speechless.

"Oh, Tony Randall in my shop! I never thought! Oh, would you talk to my wife? She's such a fan of yours."

He flattered me so that I bought three ties and a couple of shirts, I didn't have enough money and when I asked him if he'd take a check he said, "Have you got any identification?"

—Tony Randall

I love that if you have a crush on a boy, you can call your agent and get to meet him. That's probably the biggest perk.

—Claire Danes

I was playing music in the 50s and man, it was all I did. It saved my life. I'm not a hermit. Exclusive, maybe, but not reclusive.

—Bob Dylan

A lot of people say, "How does it feel to be in the Rock and Roll Hall of Fame?" I don't feel nothing, I was just doing something I like doing.

—Ike Turner

I think the [Mamas & the Papas] was a little bubble of energy that had its moment in space, and then it exhausted itself. Like those Supernovas, it burned itself out.

—Michelle Phillips

I don't want to complain about it, but there are a lot of pressures. You go to town and people want a good show. They don't care whether you did a good show last night or you do a good show tomorrow night. They want to see a good show that night. And they deserve it. They worked hard for their money and they put it down. And so you've got this pressure to perform....You got limos, you got the police escorts screaming up through the town. Everyone makes a big deal that Led Zeppelin is in town, and it's unreal. Some people deal with it in different ways. The way I dealt with it was trying to be like a little island of normality.

—John Paul Jones

I've always been a sucker for attention.

–Cuba Gooding, Jr.

I find that fame tends to turn one from an actor and a human being into a piece of merchandise, a public institution. Well, I don't intend to undergo that metamorphosis. This is why I fight so tenaciously to protect my privacy, to keep interviews like this one to an absolutely minimum, to fend off prying photographers who want to follow me around and publicize my every step and every breath.

–Sean Connery

We thought that if we lasted for two to three years that would be fantastic.

–Ringo Starr

I don't even want to be just the best. I want to grow so tall that nobody can reach me...

–James Dean

Everyone wants to be Cary Grant. Even I want to be Cary Grant.

–Cary Grant

Fame is fickle and I know it. It has its compensations, but it also has its drawbacks and I've experienced them both.

–Marilyn Monroe

They really did tell me I had no talent and I'd never get any-where. I should get all my money back from that place.

–**Sigourney Weaver**

I won't be happy until I'm as famous as God.

–**Madonna**

Don't Drink the Water

or eat the food

☆ ☆ ☆ ☆ ☆ ☆ ☆ ☆

The second day of a diet is always easier than the first. By the second day you're off it.

—Jackie Gleason

I never worry about diets. The only carrots that interest me are the number you get in a diamond.

—Mae West

I proudly say I'm a size 24. . . I could eat just legumes, but I really, really don't want a life without tiramisu.

—Camryn Manheim

At meals I'd eat a little chicken breast, maybe a little scoop of rice. It's all about portions; nothing was bigger than the palm of my hand.

—Tom Hanks on losing weight for *Castaway*

I prefer Hostess fruit pies to pop-up toaster tarts because they don't require so much cooking.

—Carrie Snow

I grew up eating well. Cheese grits, homemade biscuits smothered in butter, home-cured ham, red-eyed gravy—and that was just breakfast...Food was the guest of honor, covering so much of the tables there was hardly room for plates.

−Oprah Winfrey

I've noticed the customers in health-food stores. They are pale, skinny people who usually look half dead. In a steak house, you see robust, ruddy people. They're dying of course, but they look terrific.

−Bill Cosby

Red meat is not bad for you. Now blue-green meat, that's bad for you!

−Tommy Smothers

A nuclear power plant is infinitely safer than eating, because 300 people choke to death on food every year.

−Dixy Lee Ray

They say hot dogs can kill you. How do you know it's not the buns?

−Jay Leno

Electricity is actually made up of extremely tiny particles called electrons, that you cannot see with the naked eye unless you have been drinking.

−Dave Barry

Tequila. Straight. There's a real polite drink. You keep drinking until you finally take one more and it just won't go down. Then you know you've reached your limit.

–Lee Marvin

Gimme a whiskey, ginger ale on the side...and don't be stingy, baby!

–Greta Garbo in *Anna Christie*

Ovaltine...why do they call it Ovaltine?? The mug is round, the jar is round...they should call it Roundtine...

–Jerry Seinfeld

If there's anything unsettling to the stomach, it's watching actors on television talk about their personal lives.

–Marlon Brando

My doctor told me to stop having intimate dinners for four, Unless there are three other people.

–Orson Welles

A hot dog at the ballpark is better than a steak at the Ritz.

–Humphrey Bogart

...behind the whole process—the shopping, the planning, preparing, the serving—cooking is really about love. Cooking is a way to show it, share it, serve it. Cooking is as much about nourishment for the soul as it is for the stomach.

–Patti LaBelle

Good food shared with family and friends is one of the real pleasures in life.

−Kenny Rogers

The embarrassing thing is that my salad dressing is out-grossing my films.

−Paul Newman

I think the hardest thing is losing weight. That's the hardest thing more than anything else.

−Aretha Franklin

Health nuts are going to feel stupid someday, lying in hospitals dying of nothing.

−Redd Foxx

For breakfast I had two bowls of Sugar Puffs, for lunch two chicken fillets with loads of vegetables. I'm eating some cod and more vegetables now, and when I get home my mum will have a dinner ready. Now does that sound like a woman with a weight problem to you?

−Posh Spice

What contemptible scoundrel has stolen the cork to my lunch?

−W. C. Fields

I don't drink. I don't like it. It makes me feel good.

−Oscar Levant

As life's pleasures go, food is second only to sex. Except for salami and eggs. Now that's better than sex, but only if the salami is thickly sliced.

— **Alan King**

It's okay to be fat. So you're fat. Just be fat and shut up about it.

— **Roseanne Barr**

I know a man who gave up smoking, drinking, sex, and rich food. He was healthy right up to the time he killed himself.

— **Johnny Carson**

I love food. My favorite thing to do in the world is eat. Absolutely... Everything. If it doesn't eat me first, I'll eat it. Japanese food is my favorite, and steak. I love taking a woman to dinner, and I love watching her enjoy her food. And I love the way girls look in restaurants—lighting and candles, and the way women hold their silverware, and the way they chew their food. It's just a very sexy thing to me, and I've always liked it.

— **Freddie Prinze, Jr.**

[My favorite foods are] Almost anything Japanese, but certainly sushi above all.

— **Pierce Brosnan**

Dessert is probably the most important stage of the meal, since it will be the last thing your guests remember before they pass out all over the table.

— **William Powell**

I hate it when people come up to me when I'm eating.

−Shirley Bassey

If I could live my life over again, there is one thing I would change. I would want to be able to eat less.

−Luciano Pavarotti

You don't eat Oreos? The way you break 'em open and.... It's like you're having sex with 'em.

−Kramer in *Seinfeld*

My idea of heaven is a great big baked potato and someone to share it with.

−Oprah Winfrey

I feel sorry for people who don't drink. When they wake up in the morning, that's as good as they're going to feel all day.

−Frank Sinatra

The reason there are two senators for each state is so that one can be the designated driver.

−Jay Leno

Conversation is the enemy of good wine and food.

−Alfred Hitchcock

I have to think hard to name an interesting man who does not drink.

−Richard Burton

I can't postpone my life until I lose weight. I have to live right now.

—**Delta Burke**

I try not to eat more than I can lift.

—**Miss Piggy**

Everything you see I owe to spaghetti.

—**Sophia Loren**

I'm addicted to Altoids. I call them "acting pills."

—**Harrison Ford**

I don't drink anymore...I freeze it and eat it like a popsicle.

—**Dean Martin**

Health food may be good for the conscience but Oreos taste a hell of a lot better.

—**Robert Redford**

I start off every morning with a healthy breakfast, usually cereal and eggs. The rest of my day consists of small meals high in protein and low in complex carbs.

—**Melissa Etheridge**

I read about the evils of drinking, so I gave up reading.

—**Henny Youngman**

Researchers have discovered that chocolate produces some of the same reactions in the brain as marijuana. The researchers also discovered other similarities between the two but can't remember what they are.

−Matt Lauer (on NBC's *Today Show*)

I was a vegetarian until I started leaning toward the sunlight.

−Rita Rudner

All I really need is love, but a little chocolate now and then doesn't hurt.

−Lucy Van Pelt, *Peanuts*

We are living in a world today where lemonade is made from artificial flavors and furniture polish is made from real lemons.

−Alfred E. Newman

I like my coffee like I like my women. In a plastic cup.

−Eddie Izzard

I went to a restaurant that serves "breakfast at any time." So I ordered French toast during the Renaissance.

−Steven Wright

Did you ever notice they never take any fat hostages? You never see a guy coming out of Lebanon going: I was held hostage for seven months and I lost 175 pounds, I feel good and I look good, and I learned self-discipline. That's the important thing.

−Denis Leary

During the making of *Giant*, Rock [Hudson] and I hit it off right away...during our toots, we concocted the best drink I ever tasted—a chocolate martini made with vodka, Hershey's syrup, and Kahlua. How we survived I'll never know.

—Elizabeth Taylor

Without question, the greatest invention in the history of mankind is beer. Oh, I grant you that the wheel was also a fine invention, but the wheel does not go nearly as well with pizza.

—Dave Barry

I'm for anything that gets you through the night, be it prayer, tranquilizers or a bottle of Jack Daniels.

—Frank Sinatra

I'm a salty, greasy girl. I give every French fry a fair chance. Could you just lay some lard on my belly?

—Cameron Diaz

I've mastered the art of rice—they say anyone can cook rice, but few people cook it well....I've learned to make bread, which I was thrilled with. I took a Polaroid of my first bread.

—John Lennon

Lunch is for wimps.

—Oliver Stone

When I played drunks I had to remain sober because I didn't know how to play them when I was drunk.

- Richard Burton

Wherever there are bagels, there are also English muffins, bran muffins, and toast, and I'm more familiar with that. Bagels always seemed quite tough when you looked at them.

- Charlton Heston

Come on. I got drunk when I was like 5.

- Fiona Apple on turning 21

I was more and more aware of the fact that I was keeping my singing job to buy beer. I mean, I was sitting there doing other people's music because it made me happy, and now I was miserable, just utterly empty.

- Mary-Chapin Carpenter

I now realize that taking drugs was like taking an aspirin without having a headache.

- Paul McCartney

Green Eggs and Ham was the story of my life. I wouldn't eat a thing when I was a kid, but Dr. Seuss inspired me to try cauliflower.

- Jim Carrey

My diet is extraordinary perhaps only from the viewpoint of my close friends, who have named me "the scavenger" because, after finishing every morsel of my own meal, I look around to purloin whatever little delicacies they've left uneaten on *their* plates. Being a good leaver is practically a requisite for any friend who is invited to luncheon or to dine with me.

–**Cary Grant**

My sister gave me a big bucket of Cool Whip [for Christmas]. Isn't that awesome? For two weeks I basically watched *Emergency!* and ate cool whip with a spoon.

–**Steve Zahn**

You can't drown yourself in drink. I've tried; you float.

–**John Barrymore**

I like to eat well because I feel better but I'm not obsessed with that.

–**Penelope Cruz**

Anything is good if it's made of chocolate.

–**Jo Brand**

The perfect lover is one who turns into pizza at 4 A.M.

–**Charles Pierce**

As a child my family's menu consisted of two choices: take it or leave it.

–**Buddy Hackett**

...macaroni and cheese....It gives you cellulite. It sticks to your intestines and makes you constipated, but I love it and I'd never give it up.

—Drew Barrymore

...food meant security and comfort. Food meant love. It didn't matter what you ate, just that you had enough. I've paid a heavy price for believing that.

—Oprah Winfrey

It's A Wonderful Life

if you know how to live it

☆ ☆ ☆ ☆ ☆ ☆ ☆ ☆

Humor is just another defense against the universe.
—**Mel Brooks**

Mistakes are part of the dues one pays for a full life.
—**Sophia Loren**

Every silver lining's got a touch of grey.
—**The Grateful Dead**

Speak up for yourself, or you'll end up a rug.
—**Mae West**

If you let your head get too big, it'll break your neck.
—**Elvis Presley**

Dream as if you'll live forever. Live as if you'll die today.
—**James Dean**

Instant gratification takes too long.

–Carrie Fisher

If you want a guarantee, buy a toaster.

–Clint Eastwood

The absolute truth is the thing that makes people laugh.

–Carl Reiner

There are things to confess that enrich the world, and things that need not be said.

–Joni Mitchell

Seeing is not always believing.

–Rod Serling

I don't like driving very much. That makes me very unhappy, because I scream a lot in the car, but other than that, life is actually pretty good.

–Whoopi Goldberg

I realized that if what we call human nature can be changed, then absolutely anything is possible. From that moment, my life changed.

–Shirley MacLaine

You can have it all. You just can't have it all at one time.

–Oprah Winfrey

For fast-acting relief try slowing down.

–Lily Tomlin

To me, country music is a soundtrack for the lives of working people.

—**Travis Tritt**

I think the two most difficult things to deal with in life are failure and success.

—**David Lee Roth**

You can't be brave if you've only had wonderful things happen to you.

—**Mary Tyler Moore**

You can't have a light without a dark to stick it in.

—**Arlo Guthrie**

Music is your own experiences, your own thoughts, your own wisdom. If you don't live it, it won't come out of your horn. They teach you there's a boundary line to music. But, man there's no boundary line to art.

—**Charlie Parker**

Dress simply. If you wear a dinner jacket don't wear anything else on it...like lunch or dinner.

—**George Burns**

Education is when you read the fine print. Experience is what you get if you don't.

—**Pete Seeger**

Between two evils, I always choose the one I never tried before.

—**Mae West**

You've got to make haste while it's still light of day. My god-mother used to say, "I don't want to rust out, I just want to work out."

—Ben Vereen

Better to burn out than rust out.

—Neil Young

The best revenge is massive success.

—Frank Sinatra

You can't expect to hit the jackpot if you don't put a few nickels in the machine.

—Flip Wilson

Talk low, talk slow, and don't say too much.

—John Wayne

There are things known, and there are things unknown. And in between are the doors.

—Jim Morrison

The most important thing a man can know is that, as he approaches his own door, someone on the other side is listening for the sound of his footsteps.

—Clark Gable

Always continue the climb. It is possible for you to do whatever you choose, if you first get to know who you are and are willing to work with a power that is greater than ourselves to do it.

—Oprah Winfrey

You've got to have something to eat and a little love in your life before you can hold still for any damn body's sermon on how to behave.

−Billie Holiday

I would advise you to keep your overhead down; avoid a major drug habit; play everyday, and take it in front of other people. They need to hear it, and you need them to hear it.

−James Taylor

Life is like a B-picture script! It is that corny. If I had my life story offered to me to film, I'd turn it down.

−Kirk Douglas

Never burn bridges. Today's junior jerk, tomorrow's senior partner.

−Sigourney Weaver

You can't just sit there and wait for people to give you that golden dream. You've got to get out there and make it happen for yourself.

−Diana Ross

No matter how big or soft your bed is, you still have to get out of it.

−Grace Slick

I'm locked in my own world. I spend all my time in my basement. I rarely come out of there except for meals.

−Howard Stern

No matter how cynical you become, it's never enough to keep up.

–Lily Tomlin

Don't carry a grudge. While you're carrying the grudge, the other guy's out dancing.

–Buddy Hackett

Life is what happens to us while we are making other plans.

–John Lennon

If you obey all the rules, you miss all the fun.

–Katharine Hepburn

If you haven't good stories to tell on your deathbed, what good was living?

–Sandra Bullock

It is useless to hold a person to anything he says while he's in love, drunk, or running for office.

–Shirley MacLaine

The thing is to be able to outlast the trends.

–Paul Anka

Truth is like the sun. You can shut it out for a time, but it ain't goin' away.

–Elvis Presley

Trying to grow up is hurting, you know. You make mistakes. You try to learn from them, and when you don't, it hurts even more.

–Aretha Franklin

Don't think for a moment that I'm really like any of the characters I've played. I'm not. That's why it's called "acting."

—**Leonardo DiCaprio**

Comedy is simply a funny way of being serious.

—**Peter Ustinov**

Freedom's just another word for nothing left to lose.

—**Kris Kristofferson**

Love yourself first and everything else falls into line. You really have to love yourself to get anything done in this world

—**Lucille Ball**

I've always said that if anyone ever thought I was straight they must need glasses—but when I finally came out and said, "Yes, I do sleep with men and I'm gay," yeah, I lost record sales.

—**Boy George**

Remember, if you ever need a helping hand, it's at the end of your arm, as you get older, remember you have another hand: The first is to help yourself, the second is to help others.

—**Audrey Hepburn**

You may be disappointed if you fail, but you are doomed if you don't try.

—**Beverly Sills**

There is nothing like a challenge to bring out the best in a man.

—**Sean Connery**

Excellence I can reach for, perfection is God's business.

–Michael J. Fox

To err is human—but it feels divine.

–Mae West

There can be no liberty that isn't earned.

–Robert Young

You can do one of two things; just shut up, which is something I don't find easy, or learn an awful lot very fast, which is what I tried to do.

–Jane Fonda

A man's got to know his limitations.

–Clint Eastwood

I had to learn to look out for myself when I was a kid. I had no one to talk to. I was all alone. It taught me to be self-reliant.

–Steve McQueen

Just remember, we're all in this alone.

–Lily Tomlin

In order to have great happiness, you have to have great pain and unhappiness—otherwise how would you know when you're happy?

–Leslie Caron

It's all right letting yourself go as long as you can let yourself back.

–Mick Jagger

If you're smart, you'll always be humble. You can learn all you want, but there'll always be somebody who's never read a book who'll know twice what you know.

− David Duchovny

You've got to enjoy the moment but equally try and work so that it keeps going. You can't rush it, and you don't want to create problems for yourself. I've got to take some time out and take stock, choose what I want to do next carefully.

− Jude Law

Sometimes you have to let people down in order to get on, particularly in show business.

− Dusty Springfield

How well I have learned that there is no fence to sit on between heaven and hell. There is a deep, wide gulf, a chasm, and in that chasm is no place for any man.

− Johnny Cash

There's a period of life when we swallow a knowledge of ourselves and it becomes either good or sour inside.

− Pearl Bailey

You can be true to the character all you want but you've got to go home with yourself.

− Julia Roberts

Fast is fine, but accuracy is everything.

− Wyatt Earp

People seldom do what they believe in. They do what is convenient, then repent.

—**Bob Dylan**

The high note is the only thing.

—**Placido Domingo**

Stay humble. Always answer the phone, no matter who else is in the car.

—**Jack Lemmon**

The only thing which is important in life is karma, which roughly means actions. Every action has a reaction, which is equal and opposite.

—**George Harrison**

People think the film industry is going to corrupt me, but it's kept me more innocent. I wasn't home when my friends were trying pot for the first time.

—**Natalie Portman**

I live for myself and I answer to nobody.

—**Steve McQueen**

There is more stupidity than hydrogen in the universe. And it has a longer shelf life.

—**Frank Zappa**

Tragedy is when I cut my finger. Comedy is when you fall down an open manhole cover and die.

—**Mel Brooks**

When the going gets rough, you are obviously in the wrong place.
—**Miss Piggy**

Knowledge speaks, but wisdom listens.
—**Jimi Hendrix**

I'm not into working out. My philosophy: No pain, no pain.
—**Carol Leifer**

What the hell—you may be right, might be wrong...but don't just avoid.
—**Katharine Hepburn**

Trust your husband, adore your husband, and get as much as you can in your own name.
—**Joan Rivers**

Start every day off with a smile and get it over with.
—**W. C. Fields**

If you're going to be able to look back on something and laugh about it, you might as well laugh about it now.
—**Marie Osmond**

... everyone's got a right to his own opinion. I believe that. And I also believe that you can't make everyone like you, no matter who you are.
—**Elvis Presley**

Reality is just a crutch for people who can't cope with drugs.
— **Lily Tomlin**

Some men rob you with a six-gun—others rob you with a fountain pen.
— **Woody Guthrie**

Don't compromise yourself. You are all you've got.
— **Janis Joplin**

Life is a great big canvas, and you should throw all the paint you can on it.
— **Danny Kaye**

I think education is power. I think that being able to communicate with people is power. One of my main goals on the planet is to encourage people to empower themselves.
— **Oprah Winfrey**

Never go to bed mad. Stay up and fight.
— **Phyllis Diller**

Smoking kills. If you're killed, you've lost a very important part of your life.
— **Brooke Shields**

Attempt the impossible in order to improve your work.
— **Bette Davis**

It's not the having, it's the getting.

—Elizabeth Taylor

The only thing experience teaches you is what you can't do. When you start, you think you can do anything. And then you start to get a little tired.

—Elaine May

A few years ago, I would have told you that it should have happened for me then. But I'm glad it happened this way. It does give me more perspective. I'd like to think that way, anyway.

—Matt Damon

I quite like mistakes. I think they're human.

—Sting

I think the prime reason for existence, for living in this world is discovery.

—James Dean

Don't try to be like Jackie. There is only one Jackie... Study computers instead.

—Jackie Chan

Don't do drugs, don't have unprotected sex, don't be violent. Leave that to me.

—Eminem

I used golf as a Zen exercise....I learned that a person who is able to concentrate and focus can do almost anything.

—T Bone Burnett

In society's present stage of evolution, how can anyone tell anyone else how best to live? I can only advise you to relax and, just as all lasting religions prescribe, have faith in a master plan far greater than our minds can yet perceive. Find, through prayer, an inner peace for yourself no matter what goes on around you.

—Cary Grant

I'm just trying to make a smudge on the collective unconscious.

—David Letterman

It's the moment you think you can't that you realize you can.

—Celine Dion

Humor, you can't exist without it. You have to be able to laugh at yourself. Otherwise, you suffer.

—Kirk Douglas

Initially I wanted to be Muhammed Ali. But then I got into a fight and I got my butt kicked, so I figured I could choose something else.

—Kenneth "Babyface" Edmonds

Even from a very early age, I knew I didn't want to miss out on anything life had to offer just because it might be considered dangerous.

–Nicole Kidman

I think every American actor wants to be a movie star. But I never wanted to do stupid movies, I wanted to do films. I vowed I would never do a commercial, nor would I do a soap opera–both of which I did as soon as I left the [Acting Company] and was starving.

–Kevin Kline

May you live as long as you want and not want as long as you live.

–Tom Hanks

Laughter gives us distance. It allows us to step back from an event, deal with it and then move on.

–Bob Newhart

I should've known then what show business was about – but I stayed on stage.

–Olympia Dukakis

Instead of always looking at the past, I put myself ahead twenty years and try to look at what I need to do now in order to get there then.

–Diana Ross

The more sensitive you are, the more likely you are to be brutalized, develop scabs and never evolve. Never allow yourself to feel anything because you always feel too much.

–Marlon Brando

I have to act to live.

–Lawrence Olivier

My travels led me to where I am today. Sometimes these steps have felt painful, difficult, but led me to greater happiness and opportunities.

–Diana Ross

I place a high moral value on the way people behave. I find it repellent to have a lot, and to behave with anything other than courtesy in the old sense of the word–politeness of the heart, a gentleness of the spirit.

–Emma Thompson

Just because nobody complains doesn't mean all parachutes are perfect

–Benny Hill

When music fails to agree to the ear, to soothe the ear and the heart and the senses, then it has missed its point.

–Maria Callas

People do not live nowadays. They get about ten percent out of life.
—Isadora Duncan

We cast away priceless time in dreams, born of imagination, fed upon illusion, and put to death by reality.
—Judy Garland

My life has been a series of emergencies.
—Lana Turner

Listening is being able to be changed by the other person.
—Alan Alda

You can cage the singer but not the song.
—Harry Belafonte

You have to be fairly selfish when you have a gift. You cannot afford to let too many outside things get in the way.
—Sarah Brightman

It's said in Hollywood that you should always forgive your enemies—because you never know when you'll have to work with them.
—Lana Turner

Blind faith in your leader, or in anything, will get you killed.
—Bruce Springsteen

Take your work seriously, but never yourself.
—**Margot Fonteyn**

Getting ahead in a difficult profession requires avid faith in yourself. That is why some people with mediocre talent, but with great inner drive, go so much further than people with vastly superior talent.
—**Sophia Loren**

Somebody once said we never know what is enough until we know what's more than enough.
—**Billie Holiday**

Never keep up with the Joneses. Drag them down to your level. It's cheaper.
—**Quentin Crisp**

If I'm going to Hell, I'm going there playing the piano.
—**Jerry Lee Lewis**

I can't do anything outside of what I'm capable of, bring my own energy, my own qualities and just work really hard. At some point, it's out of my hands.
—**Charlie Sheen**

No one can dub you with dignity. That's yours to claim.
—**Odetta**

I'm incredibly open as a person. I'm a believer rather than a disbeliever. But I'm not particularly interested in knowing the future. I'd rather let life unfold.

–Cate Blanchett

Anything can happen to anyone at any time and you shouldn't just live through the days, or you lose them. You should do what you can to enjoy every moment.

–Sarah Brightman

You have to leave room in life to dream.

–Buffy Sainte-Marie

Challenges make you discover things about yourself that you never really knew. They're what make the instrument stretch – what make you go beyond the norm.

–Cicely Tyson

You name it and I've done it. I'd like to say I did it my way. But that line, I'm afraid, belongs to someone else.

–Sammy Davis, Jr.

The body is your instrument in dance, but your art is outside that creature, the body.

–Martha Graham

I was like the Energizer bunny, and I needed to slow down.

–Halle Berry

Whatever you want to do, do it now. There are only so many tomorrows.

–Michael Landon

We all have Hitler in us, but we also have love and peace. So why not give peace a chance for once?

–John Lennon

Sometimes the road less traveled is less traveled for a reason.

–Jerry Seinfeld

Flops are a part of life's menu and I've never been a girl to miss out on any of the courses.

–Rosalind Russell

There are some good people [in Hollywood]. But a good chunk of them will lie for no reason at all–it'll be ten o'clock and they'll tell you it's nine. You're looking at the clock and you can't even fathom why they're lying. They just lie because that's what they do.

–John Cusack

You must learn to say no when something is not right for you.

–Leontyne Price

Kids are at my level. I like goofing around with them.

–John Goodman

You don't get to choose how you're going to die. Or when. You can decide how you're going to live now.
– Joan Baez

I need to get the sex back in my acting!
– Demi Moore

Never continue in a job you don't enjoy. If you're happy in what you're doing, you'll like yourself, you'll have inner peace. And I you have that, along with physical health, you will have had more success than you could possibly have imagined.
– Johnny Carson

It takes a lot of guts to get up on top of a bar and dance.
– Piper Perabo

I really lived life to its fullest and that got me in trouble from time to time.
– Matthew Perry

I decided if I walk outside and get hit by a bus, everybody'll say, "He crammed a load into 34 years."
– George Clooney

Only a genius can play a fool.
– Michael Rapaport

You can't undo the past... but you can certainly not repeat it.
– Bruce Willis

I don't have high expectations anymore. Maybe they've just been beaten out of me.
— Elisabeth Shue

It's hard to follow my own act. But the only answer to that would be to give up after the Beatles. I only had two alternatives. Give up or carry on.
— Paul McCartney

The way I see things, the way I see life, I see it as a struggle. And there's a great deal of reward I have gained coming to that understanding—that existence is a struggle.
— Harvey Keitel

While we have the gift of life, it seems to me the only tragedy is to allow part of us to die—whether it is our spirit, our creativity, or our glorious uniqueness.
— Gilda Radner

I don't really think about anything too much. I live in the present. I move on. I don't think about what happened yesterday. If I think too much, it kind of freaks me out.
— Pamela Anderson

My theory is that if you look confident you can pull off anything—even if you have no clue what you're doing.
— Jessica Alba

I can't decide whether to commit suicide or go bowling.
— Florence Henderson

Not only is there no God, but try finding a plumber on Sunday.
– **Woody Allen**

My message here, is: If you are unhappy with anything—your mother, your father, your husband, your wife, your job, your boss, your car—whatever is bringing you down, get rid of it. Because you'll find that when you're free, your true creativity, your true self comes out.
– **Tina Turner**

[Federico Fellini] was always asking me who the hell I thought I was. I was always trying to find out.
– **Anthony Quinn**

The view, of course, isn't always so glorious. After all those years of broken promises and pulled-out rugs, I've gotten used to expecting an ambush around every corner. This is the entertainment business, after all. The faces change but the nature of the beast doesn't.
– **Darlene Love**

Even if you're not someone who is successful and young in Hollywood, my guess is that almost everyone goes through a very rocky period of adjustment in their life. But if you're in the public eye when it happens, the tendency is to never let you forget your mistakes.
– **Rob Lowe**

I wasn't as smart then as I am now. But who ever is?
– **Tina Turner**

We each have our own vision and a voice inside that talks only to us. We have to be able to hear it.

— **Bob Dylan**

I believe a man writes the story of his life not in order to remember, but in order to forget. I was never the same man from one day to the next, which is perhaps why I am desperate to know the man I have become, finally. This is it. I have lived in a flurry of images, but I will go out in a freeze frame.

— **Anthony Quinn**

If you lose your demons, you lose your angels, or so I used to think. But that doesn't scare me anymore. My demons are always going to be there. They're along for the ride. I just spent a lot less time hanging out with them than I used to. These days I prefer chatting with my angels.

— **Kelsey Grammer**

Television? Not for me, thank you. It had been hard enough to come out of hiding and play *Voice of the Turtle*. Take on a full-time job in a medium that didn't amount to anything? The strain involved wasn't worth it. Besides, what could it lead to? No series anything like *I Love Lucy* had ever been successful so far.

— **Vivian Vance**

I'm never really balanced in the middle. I go from one side to the other without staying in either place very long. I'm happy, sad, up, down, in, out, up in the sky and down in the depths of the earth. I can't tell you how Bob Dylan has lived his life. And it's far from over.

–Bob Dylan

Never face facts; if you do you'll never get up in the morning.

–Marlo Thomas

In the end, everything is a gag.

–Charlie Chaplin

The trouble with being in the rat race is that even if you win, you're still a rat.

–Lily Tomlin

There will be no nuclear war. There's too much real estate involved.

–Frank Zappa

There's something about death that is comforting. The thought you could die tomorrow frees you to appreciate your life now.

–Angelina Jolie

The only thing I regret about my life is the length of it. If I had to live my life again, I'd make all the same mistakes—only sooner.

–Tallulah Bankhead

Be nice to your children, for they will choose your rest home.
–**Phyllis Diller**

Hope for the best. Expect the worst. Life is a play. We're unrehearsed.
–**Mel Brooks**

Love is a Many-Splendored Thing

so is sex, but marriage?

☆ ☆ ☆ ☆ ☆ ☆ ☆ ☆

If it's true that men are such beasts—this must account for the fact that most women are animal lovers.

—Farrah Fawcett

Don't have sex man. It leads to kissing and pretty soon you have to start talking to them.

—Steve Martin

I believe in the institution of marriage and I intend to keep trying until I get it right.

—Richard Pryor

I have loved many men, but have never been in love with any of them. I never had the time.

—Lillian Gish

I heard there was a lot of porno stuff on the Web. I looked for it and couldn't find it. Then I found this one site and it was twenty bucks a month! Twenty bucks a month! *Hustler's* only $3.99.

−**Ben Affleck**

Generally women are better than men—they have more character. I prefer men for some things, obviously, but women have a greater sense of honor and are more willing to take a chance with their lives. They are more open and decent in their relationship with a man. Men run all the time. I don't know how they live with themselves, they are so preoccupied with being studs.

−**Lauren Bacall**

I believe in using words, not fists...I believe in my outrage knowing people are living in boxes on the street...I believe in honesty. I believe in a good time. I believe in good food. I believe in sex.

−**Susan Sarandon**

Thank God for the tolerance shown to me by ladies with whom I've had long stretches because I'm quite hopeless with women. I've tried, and even succeeded in, living with a woman but it's never satisfactory, certainly not for her. I'm a loner. Living with someone is not for me.

−**Peter O'Toole**

Once you start having on-screen sex, it isn't embarrassing anymore.

−**Annette Bening**

I might not be a great actress but I've become the greatest at screen orgasms. Ten seconds of heavy breathing, roll your head from side to side, simulate a slight asthma attack, and die a little.

–Candice Bergen

If I'm not interested in a woman, I'm straight-forward. Right after sex, I usually say, "I can't do this anymore. Thanks for coming over."

–Vince Vaughn

A bit of lusting after someone does wonders for the skin.

–Elizabeth Hurley

Is sex dirty? Only if it's done right.

–Woody Allen

Dating is pressure and tension. What is a date, really, but a job interview that lasts all night? The only difference between a date and a job interview is that in not many job interviews is there a chance you'll end up naked at the end of it.

–Jerry Seinfeld

I wish I had as much in bed as I get in the newspapers.

–Linda Ronstadt

A man can sleep around, no questions asked; but if a woman makes nineteen or twenty mistakes she's a tramp.

–Joan Rivers

No rich man is ugly.

– Zsa Zsa Gabor

A nuclear reactor is just like a woman, all you have to do is read the manual and push the right buttons.

– Homer Simpson

I know that my fans want to know who I'm sleeping with, but it's really none of their business.

– Diana Ross

These days I am sleeping alone. Sometimes I wake up in the middle of the night, put on my blue eye shadow and try to learn country dancing in front of the TV.

– Cybill Shepherd

People think that I act sexy but if you speak to my backing dancers, they say I am a prude. I won't allow certain movements and I won't allow too much show. I'd say I am quite old-fashioned.

– Tina Turner

There's this illusion that homosexuals have sex and heterosexuals fall in love. That's completely untrue. Everybody wants to be loved.

– Boy George

Don't knock masturbation, it's sex with someone I love.

– Woody Allen

In Spain, there's the king–and then there's Antonio.

– Melanie Griffith

I fell in love with her [Melanie Griffith]—and to describe that, you would have to be a poet. I don't know if you can describe when two people fall in love. But it wasn't love at first sight. We were working on the same movie [Two Much], and little by little, it was happening. When we finished, we said goodbye to each other. Then we just hung out on the phone for a long time.

—Antonio Banderas

Diamonds never leave you ... men do!

—Shirley Bassey

I'm just looking for that moment to drop my Jedi knickers and pull out my real light saber.

—Ewan McGregor

When I go out with the ladies, I don't force them to pronounce my name. I tell them I like to go by the nickname Kitten.

—Joaquin Phoeniz

I've gone for each type: the rough guy; the nerdy, sweet, lovable guy; and the slick guy. I don't really have a type. Men in general are a good thing.

—Jennifer Aniston

Chains do not hold a marriage together. It is threads, hundreds of tiny threads which sew people together through the years. That is what makes a marriage last—more than passion or even sex!

—Simone Signoret

Husbands think we should know where everything is: like the uterus is a tracking device. He asks me, "Roseanne, do we have any Cheetos left?" Like he can't go over to that sofa cushion and lift it himself.

—**Roseanne Barr**

My parents' divorce made me want to make my marriage work.

—**Denzel Washington**

I've got a good man. He takes care of me. I don't have to be scared of anything because I know he will kick every ass ... disrespect him and you've got a problem.

—**Whitney Houston**

When he's late for dinner, I know he's either having an affair or is lying dead in the street. I always hope it's the street.

—**Jessica Tandy**

There was a lot of tabloid journalism about my supposed sex addiction. Bullshit. It's all bullshit. I mean, come on, I never pretended to be a saint. But give me a break.

—**Michael Douglas**

If I get married, I want to be very married.

—**Audrey Hepburn**

I'm not the type of guy who enjoys one-night stands. It leaves me feeling very empty and cynical. It's not even fun sexually. I need to

feel something for the woman and entertain the vain hope that it may lead to a relationship.
– **Ben Affleck**

Believe me, the first state that legalizes same sex marriages, I'm there, Julie's there, and we're getting married. We're first in line.
– **Melissa Etheridge**

Marriages and relationships get stuck, you know? Sometimes you can crack out of it and sometimes you can't.
– **Dennis Quaid**

They tell me that it will be hard to find a man strong enough to love my own strength and independence, and not worry about being Mr. Diana Ross, but I disagree. I know absolutely that that man is somewhere out there.
– **Diana Ross**

I have such poor vision I can date anybody.
– **Garry Shandling**

I have tried sex with both men and women. I found I liked it.
– **Dusty Springfield**

As far as I'm concerned, being any gender at all is a drag.
– **Patti Smith**

I wonder why men can get serious at all. They have this delicate long thing hanging outside their bodies, which goes up and down by its own will...If I were a man I would always be laughing at myself.

– Yoko Ono

If sex is such a natural phenomenon, how come there are so many books on how to do it?

– Bette Midler

I have never liked sex. I do not think I ever will. It seems just the opposite of love.

– Marilyn Monroe

Seems to me the basic conflict between men and women, sexually, is that men are like firemen. To men, sex is an emergency, and no matter what we're doing we can be ready in two minutes. Women, on the other hand, are like fire. They're very exciting, but the conditions have to be exactly right for it to occur.

– Jerry Seinfeld

Shopping is better than sex. At least if you're not satisfied, you can exchange it for something you really like.

– Adrienne Gusoff

We had a lot in common: I loved him and he loved him.

– Shelley Winters

I had to lie so much about sex, first when I was 15, because I wasn't supposed to be having it. And then when I got older, I lied to everybody I was having sex with, so I could have sex with other people.

– Cybil Sheperd

When you are in love with someone you want to be near him all the time, except when you are out buying things and charging them to him.

–Miss Piggy

What the world really needs is more love and less paperwork.

–Pearl Bailey

I've never been married, but I tell people I'm divorced so they won't think something's wrong with me.

–Elayne Boosler

I've had diseases that lasted longer than my marriages.

–Nell Carter

In the silence of night I have often wished for just a few words of love from one man, rather than the applause of thousands of people.

–Judy Garland

The first six months of a relationship are wonderful. I love that intensity, the passion, the "can't keep away from each other," then it all starts to taper off. They don't want to stay home and watch television, they want to go out. They don't want to listen to what I say, they start putting me down and I won't take that.

–Shirley Bassey

The average man is more interested in a woman who is interested in him than he is in a woman—any woman—with beautiful legs.

–Marlene Dietrich

A gentleman is simply a patient wolf.

—Lana Turner

As she lay there dozing next to me, one voice inside my head kept saying, "Relax...you are not the first doctor to sleep with one of his patients," but another kept reminding me, "Howard, you are a veterinarian."

—Dick Wilson

I didn't know how babies were made until I was pregnant with my fourth child.

—Loretta Lynn

[Adultery.] It's a game I never play.

—Sophia Loren

I'm just afraid I'm gonna miss it all ... being married ... being a mother.

—Karen Carpenter

I can't be a wife. I'm not that sort of person. Wives have to compromise all the time.

—Sarah Brightman

Any idiot can get laid when they're famous. That's easy. It's getting laid when you're not famous that takes some talent.

—Kevin Bacon

A good place to meet men is at the dry cleaner's. These men have jobs and usually bathe.

—Rita Rudner

During sex I fantasize that I'm someone else.

– Richard Lewis

I've only slept with men I've been married to. How many women can make that claim?

– Elizabeth Taylor

The ability to enjoy your sex life is central. I don't give a shit about anything else. My obsession is total; What else is there to live for?

– Dudley Moore

After about 20 years of marriage, I'm finally starting to scratch the surface of that one [what women want]. And I think the answer lies somewhere between conversation and chocolate.

– Mel Gibson

I can always be distracted by love, but eventually I get horny for my creativity.

– Gilda Radner

When you're in a relationship, it's better to be with somebody who has an affair on you than somebody who doesn't flush the toilet.

– Uma Thurman

I'm a sex machine to both genders. It's all very exhausting. I need a lot of sleep.

– Rupert Everett

Winning a Grammy sure helped me get laid.

–Bonnie Raitt

I'm not one of those fellows that is just going to have a pseudo-middling relationship.

–Russell Crowe

Sex without love is an empty experience, but, as empty experiences go, it's one of the best.

–Woody Allen

...people don't ask me out. There is a whole intimidation factor, I don't know what it is. I have sort of surrendered to that fact and learned to accept it.

–Alyssa Milano

Being a sex symbol has to do with an attitude, not looks. Most men think it's looks, most women know otherwise.

–Kathleen Turner

I have always found strangers sexy.

–Hugh Grant

I'm too shy to express my sexual needs except over the phone to people I don't know.

–Garry Shandling

The main problem in marriage is that, for a man, sex is a hunger—like eating. If a man is hungry and can't get to a fancy French restaurant, he'll go to a hot dog stand.

–Joan Fontaine

I'm very uncomfortable with the idea of vaginas. They bother me in the same way that spiders bother some people.

—Boy George

We've got this gift of love, but love is like a precious plant. You can't just accept it and leave it in the cupboard or just think it's going to get on by itself. You've got to keep watering it. You've got to really look after it and nurture it.

—John Lennon

You can't keep it up with sixteen-year-old girls forever. They're very demanding.

—Mick Jagger

I'm good at being sarcastic with guys. They don't want the quiet, prissy little things.

—Jessica Alba

I don't think pornography is very harmful, but it is terribly, terribly boring.

—Noel Coward

I was married by a judge...I should have asked for a jury.

—George Burns

I try to remember, as I hear about friends getting engaged, that it's not about the ring. It's a great thing, getting married.

—Gwyneth Paltrow

I'm probably not going to get married unless I live with somebody for 10 or 20 years. But these people [Romeo and Juliet] took a chance and they did it. We don't have the balls that Romeo did.

−**Leonardo DiCaprio**

Some things are better than sex, and some are worse, but there's nothing exactly like it.

−**W. C. Fields**

My husband complained to me. He said, "I can't remember when we last had sex," and I said, "Well I can and that's why we ain't doing it."

−**Roseanne Barr**

It was only after I got into show business that women started to like me. Before that I wasn't popular.

−**John Travolta**

Love is so much better when you are not married.

−**Maria Callas**

Whatever I do, it's my business. It's not my job to parent America.

−**Christina Aguilera**

The homosexual community wants me to be gay. The heterosexual community wants me to be straight. Every [writer] thinks, "I'm the journalist who's going to make him talk." I pray for them. I pray that they get a life and stop living mine!

−**Ricky Martin**

I really want to love somebody. I do. I just don't know if it's possible forever and ever.

−**Jim Carrey**

At a certain point, a man wants to own you, and no man will ever own me.

−**Grace Jones**

Being married means I can [break wind] and eat ice cream in bed.

−**Brad Pitt**

I'm always described as "cocksure" or "with a swagger," and that bears no resemblance to who I feel like inside. I feel plagued by insecurity.

−**Ben Affleck**

Many a man has fallen in love with a girl in a light so dim he would not have chosen a suit by it.

−**Maurice Chevalier**

I feel like a million tonight—but one at a time.

−**Mae West**

Is it a man walking on the beach, winking at the girls and looking for going to bed? Is it someone who wears a lot of gold chains and rings and sits at the bar? Because this is not me! I am very, very Latin, but not so much lover.

−**Antonio Banderas**

I'm as confident as Cleopatra's pussy.

—Bette Midler

I like to wake up each morning feeling a new man.

—Jean Harlow

My favorite book when I was eight was *Everything You Always Wanted to Know About Sex—But Were Afraid to Ask*. I was not afraid to ask.

—Drew Barrymore

I need to get the sex back in my acting.

—Demi Moore

I'm basically a sexless geek. Look at me, I have pasty-white skin, I have acne scars and I'm five-foot-nothing. Does that sound like a real sexual dynamo to you?

—Mike Myers

When you're single again, at the beginning you're very optimistic and you say, "I want to meet someone who's really smart, really sweet, really sensitive." And six months later you're like, "Lord, any mammal with a day job."

—Carol Leifer

Using a complex, sophisticated technique to get a man excited is like preparing a gourmet French meal for a Labrador retriever.

—Dave Barry

Women need a reason to have sex—men just need a place.

–Billy Crystal

I'm as pure as the driven slush.

–Tallulah Bankhead

I used to be Snow White, but I drifted.

–Mae West

I don't like to admit it, but if a girl baited her trap with sex, she'd catch me every time—and it's unlikely this will ever cease to work.

–Willie Nelson

On stage I make love to 25,000 people; then I go home alone.

–Janis Joplin

To succeed with the opposite sex, tell her you're impotent. She can't wait to disprove it.

–Cary Grant

I never yet met a man who could look after me. I don't need a husband. What I need is a wife.

–Joan Collins

Men are creatures with two legs and eight hands.

–Jayne Mansfield

I'm such a good lover because I practice a lot on my own.

–Woody Allen

When you're in a relationship, it's better to be with somebody who has an affair on you than somebody who doesn't flush the toilet.

—Uma Thurman

Men are kind of dumb sometimes. I find women to be way smarter than men...If you want something fixed, send a man to do it. If you want someone to experience it, you'd better bring along a woman.

—Don Johnson

It's not true that I had nothing on. I had the radio on.

—Marilyn Monroe

Sex is one of the most wholesome, beautiful and natural experiences that money can buy.

—Steve Martin

My best birth control now is just to leave the lights on.

—Joan Rivers

I think people should be free to engage in any sexual practices they choose; they should draw the line at goats though.

—Elton John

They call me the Queen of the Newsstands. There are not enough hours in the day for me to do all the things they say I do, and with all the people they say I do them with.

—Cher

Sex is God's joke on human beings.

—Bette Davis

The important thing in acting is to be able to laugh and cry. If I have to cry, I think of my sex life. If I have to laugh, I think of my sex life.

—Glenda Jackson

Is it boasting to say I don't need Viagra?

—Larry King

I'm at the age where food has taken the place of sex in my life. In fact, I've just had a mirror put over my kitchen table.

—Rodney Dangerfield

A woman is an occasional pleasure but a cigar is always a smoke.

—Groucho Marx

Husbands are like fires. They go out when unattended.

—Zsa Zsa Gabor

No man worth his salt, no man of spirit and spine, no man for whom I could have any respect, could rejoice in the identification of Tallulah's husband. It's tough enough to be bogged down in a legend. It would be even tougher to marry one.

—Tallulah Bankhead

She's been on more laps than a napkin.

—Walter Winchell

He was happily married, but his wife wasn't.

–**Victor Borge**

Nothing is either all masculine or all feminine except having sex.

–**Marlo Thomas**

Think of me as a sex symbol for the men who don't give a damn.

–**Phyllis Diller**

Sex: the thing that takes up the least amount of time and causes the most amount of trouble.

–**John Barrymore**

...if you go to bed with somebody, when do you have time to read?

–**Paula Poundstone**

What's nice about my dating life is that I don't have to leave my house. All I have to do is read the paper: I'm marrying Richard Gere, dating Daniel Day-Lewis, parading around with John F. Kennedy, Jr. , and even Robert De Niro was in there for a day.

–**Julia Roberts**

What does "good in bed" mean to me? When I'm sick and I stay home from school propped up with lots of pillows watching TV and my mom brings me soup—that's good in bed.

–**Brooke Shields**

Men should be like Kleenex, soft, strong and disposable.

—**Cher**

The last thing I want is to be a 5-foot 2 guy walking down the street with a 6-foot 2 model. Like, "Look at me! Look what I can get now I got my dick caught in a zipper."

—**Ben Stiller**

I detest "love lyrics." I think one of the causes of bad mental health in the United States is that people have been raised on "love lyrics."

—**Frank Zappa**

Marriage is a great institution, but I'm not ready for an institution.

—**Mae West**

The most popular labor-saving device today is still a husband with money.

—**Joey Adams**

Marriage has absolutely changed my life. It would change anybody's. It's not the idea of marriage or being married; it's like each person is their own animal, and I found somebody who is the same breed. You are so relieved you're not the only one in the world!

—**Angelina Jolie**

When I eventually met Mr. Right I had no idea that his first name was Always.

—**Rita Rudner**

I'm looking for Miss Right, or at least, Miss Right Now.

– Robin Williams

If the income tax is the price we have to pay to keep the government on its feet, alimony is the price we have to pay for sweeping a woman off hers.

– Groucho Marx

It wasn't exactly a divorce—I was traded.

– Tim Conway

I told my wife the truth. I told her I was seeing a psychiatrist. Then she told me the truth: that she was seeing a psychiatrist, two plumbers, and a bartender.

– Rodney Dangerfield

Politics doesn't make strange bedfellows, marriage does.

– Groucho Marx

Any intelligent woman who reads the marriage contract, and then goes into it, deserves all the consequences.

– Isadora Duncan

Some people ask the secret of our long marriage. We take time to go to a restaurant two times a week. A little candlelight, dinner, soft music and dancing. She goes Tuesdays, I go Fridays.

– Henny Youngman

The truth was that with all my lipstick and mascara and precocious curves I was as unresponsive as a fossil...I used to lie awake at night wondering why the boys came after me.

–Marilyn Monroe

Losing my virginity was a career move.

–Madonna

I must quit marrying men who feel inferior to me. Somewhere there must be a man who could be my husband and not feel inferior. I need a superior inferior man.

–Hedy Lamarr

There's something sexy about a gut. Not a 400-pound beer gut, but a little paunch. I love that.

–Sandra Bullock

I'm the only man in the world with a marriage license made out "to whom it may concern."

–Mickey Rooney

Whatever you may look like, marry a man your own age—as your beauty fades, so will his eyesight.

–Phyllis Diller

I believe you have a pretty good idea [of love] right away. Although I think some people can be blind to that and can learn to find out if they love someone. But, definitely, it's quite possible to have a real good sense right away of whether it's going to work.

–Ben Affleck

I wouldn't be caught dead marrying a woman old enough to be my wife.

– Tony Curtis

Sex is hardly ever just about sex.

– Shirley MacLaine

You never realize how short a month is until you pay alimony.

– John Barrymore

The doctor must have put my pacemaker in wrong. Every time my husband kisses me, the garage door goes up.

– Minnie Pearl

If you want to sacrifice the admiration of many men for the criticism of one, go ahead, get married.

– Katharine Hepburn

Divorce is defeat.

– Lucille Ball

I've never been married, but I tell people I'm divorced so they won't think something's wrong with me.

– Elayne Boosler

One of my theories is that men love with the eyes; women love with their ears.

– Zsa Zsa Gabor

Relationships are hard to pull off even when they're at their best. When you add the outside forces that come with celebrity and fame, you almost have an unbearable pressure.

–Kevin Costner

I've had diseases that lasted longer than my marriages.

–Nell Carter

If a woman hasn't met the right man by the time she's 24, she may be lucky.

–Deborah Kerr

I earn and pay my own way as a great many women to today. Why should unmarried women be discriminated against— unmarried men are not.

–Dinah Shore

Why is it men are permitted to be obsessed about their work, but women are only permitted to be obsessed about men?

–Barbra Streisand

My husband will never chase another woman. He's too fine, too decent, too old.

–Gracie Allen

Love may not make the world go round, but I must admit that it makes the ride worthwhile.

–Sean Connery

It is better to be unfaithful than to be faithful without wanting to be.

–Brigitte Bardot

Eighty percent of married men cheat in America. The rest cheat in Europe.

–Jackie Mason

Only time can heal your broken heart, just as only time can heal his broken arms and legs.

–Miss Piggy

If you gave me a choice between the interview and the date, I would take the interview.

–Barbara Walters

A man in love is incomplete until he has married. Then he is finished.

–Zsa Zsa Gabor

I used to believe that marriage would diminish me, reduce my options. That you had to be someone less to live with someone when, of course, you have to be someone more.

–Candice Bergen

There are not withholding taxes on the wages of sin.

–Mae West

It's like when I buy a horse. I don't want a thick neck and short legs.

–Mickey Rourke

A kiss is a lovely trick designed by nature to stop speech when words become superfluous.

–Ingrid Bergman

Whenever I date a guy, I think, is this the man I want my children to spend their weekends with?

–Rita Rudner

It was so cold I almost got married.

–Shelley Winters

The only time a woman really succeeds in changing a man is when he is a baby.

–Natalie Wood

I never liked the men I loved, and never loved the men I liked.

–Fanny Brice

I've been on so many blind dates, I should get a free dog.

–Wendy Liebman

Normal love isn't interesting. I assure you that it's incredibly boring.

–Roman Polanski

A man has to be Joe McCarthy to be called ruthless. All a woman has to do is put you on hold.

–Marlo Thomas

I've been married to one Marxist and one Fascist, and neither one would take the garbage out.

—Lee Grant

Being in therapy is great. I spend an hour just talking about myself. It's kind of like being the guy on a date.

—Caroline Rhea

My grandmother's ninety. She's dating. He's ninety-three. It's great. They never argue. They can't hear each other.

—Cathy Ladman

Marriage is too interesting an experiment to be tried only once.

—Eva Gabor

My husband and I didn't sign a prenuptial agreement. We signed a mutual suicide pact.

—Roseanne Barr

Mr. Right is now a guy who hasn't been laid in fifteen years.

—Elayne Boosler

A girl can wait for the right man to come along; but in the meantime, that still doesn't mean she can't have a wonderful time with all the wrong ones.

—Cher

To attract men, I wear a perfume called "New Car Interior."

—Rita Rudner

I'm attracted to guys who are really confident and make conversation.

– Britney Spears

I'm very old-fashioned. I believe that people should marry for life, like pigeons and Catholics.

– Woody Allen

How many husbands have I had? You mean apart from my own?

– Zsa Zsa Gabor

It's like magic. When you live by yourself, all your annoying habits are gone!

– Merill Markoe

I got married for something to do. I though it was a good idea. I've never been madly, deeply in love. I wouldn't know what it feels like. I'm not really an emotional person.

– Mick Jagger

It is true that I never should have married, but I didn't want to live without a man. Brought up to respect the conventions, love had to end in marriage. I'm afraid it did.

– Bette Davis

The truth is, sex doesn't mean that much to me now.

– Lana Turner

This guy says, "I'm perfect for you, 'cause I'm a cross between a macho man and a sensitive man." I said, "Oh, a gay trucker?"

– Judy Tenuta

Two is company; three is fifty bucks.
– Joan Rivers

If love means never having to say you're sorry, then marriage means always having to say everything twice.
– Estelle Getty

I'm going to the backseat of my car with the woman I love, and I won't be back for TEN MINUTES.
– Homer Simpson in *The Simpsons*

The story of love is not important. What is important is that one is capable of love. It is perhaps the only glimpse we are permitted of eternity.
– Helen Hayes

Love is a fire. But whether it is going to warm your heart or burn down your house, you can never tell.
– Joan Crawford

It's no treat being in bed with me.
– Howard Stern

It is the ordinary women that know something about love. The gorgeous ones are too busy being gorgeous.
– Katherine Hepburn

Men who think that a woman's past love affairs lessen her love for them are usually stupid and weak. A woman can bring a new love to each man she loves, providing there are not too many.

−Marilyn Monroe

I think men are afraid to be with a successful woman, because we are terribly strong, we know what we want and we are not fragile enough.

−Shirley Bassey

The only people who make love all the time are liars.

−Louis Jordan in *Gigi*

The only men who are too young are the ones who write their love letters in crayons, wear pajamas with feet, or fly for half fare.

−Phyllis Diller

Unless there's some emotional tie, I'd rather play tennis.

−Bianca Jagger

I love you almost as much as you do.

−Walter Matthau to Jack Lemmon in *The Odd Couple*

No matter who you get married to, you wake up married to somebody else.

−Marlon Brando in *Guys and Dolls*

Before we make love my husband takes a pain killer.

−Joan Rivers

I'm always looking for meaningful one-night stands.

−Dudley Moore.

If it weren't for pickpockets, I'd have no sex life at all.

—Rodney Dangerfield

There will be sex after death; we just won't be able to feel it.

—Lily Tomlin

Yes, I'm going to be the President of the United States. You know why? You think you can get chicks by being in the movies? You can really get chicks by being the President.

—Ben Affleck

It's the good girls who keep the diaries; the bad girls never have the time.

—Tallulah Bankhead

If somebody makes me laugh, I'm his slave for life.

—Bette Midler

Brides aren't happy—they are just triumphant.

—John Barrymore

Sex when you're married is like going to a 7-Eleven. There's not much variety, but at three in the morning it's always there.

—Carol Leifer

I've sometimes thought of marrying, and then I've thought again.

—Noel Coward

I can live without money, but I cannot live without love.

—Judy Garland

The act of sex...is man's last desperate stand at superintendency.

–**Bette Davis**

Never refer to your wedding night as the "original amateur hour."

–**Phyllis Diller**

Sex appeal is 50 percent what you've got, and 50 percent what people think you've got.

–**Sophia Loren**

Men aren't necessities, they're luxuries.

–**Cher**

There's no one more depressed than a happily married man.

–**Mickey Rooney**

It's been so long since I made love, I can't even remember who gets tied up.

–**Joan Rivers**

The last time I was inside a woman was when I went to the Statue of Liberty.

–**Woody Allen,** *Crimes and Misdemeanors*

I don't pretend to be an ordinary housewife.

–**Elizabeth Taylor**

All discarded lovers should be given a second chance, but with somebody else.

–**Mae West**

Most women set out to try to change a man, and when they have changed him they don't like him.

−Marlene Dietrich

Why does a woman work ten years to change a man's habits and then complain that he's not the man she married?

−Barbra Streisand

Sometimes I wonder if men and women really suit each other. Perhaps they should live next door and just visit now and then.

−Katharine Hepburn

Women are like elephants. I like to look at 'em, but I wouldn't want to own one.

−WC Fields

My husband said he wanted to have a relationship with a red-head, so I dyed my hair red.

−Jane Fonda

I have too many fantasies to be a housewife...I guess I am a fantasy.

−Marilyn Monroe

I had a huge crush on Olga Korbut, the gymnast. The only other person was Cliff Richard, which is embarrassing−it means that when I was seven I had bad taste and was presumably gay.

−Hugh Grant

My favorite romantic couple is R2-D2 and C-3PO. They're adorable and kooky.

– Tom Hanks

It's just so horrible because I want to be in love. I look everywhere for a boyfriend. The other day, I'm looking around this bus stop for cute guys. The whole thing sucks.

– Alicia Silverstone

Why can't a woman be more like a dog, huh? So sweet, loving, attentive.

– Kirk Douglas

If I had a choice of having a woman in my arms or shooting a bad guy on a horse, I'd take the horse. It's a lot more fun.

– Kevin Costner

Marry Prince William? I would love that. After all, who wouldn't want to be a princess?

– Britney Spears

My philosophy of dating is to just fart right away.

– Jenny McCarthy

If you have intercourse, you run the risk of dying, and the ramifications of death are final.

– Cyndi Lauper

After we made love he took a piece of chalk and made an outline of my body.

– Joan Rivers

Last time I tried to make love to my wife nothing was happening, so I said to her, "What's the matter, you can't think of anybody else either?"

–Rodney Dangerfield

When I get lonely, I want to be alone. I like to indulge in my loneliness so I can figure out that I'm not really lonely.

–Alicia Silverstone

I have to be physically attracted to someone. But I can't just be with someone just because it's great sex. Because orgasms don't last long enough.

–Courtney Cox

I don't need a man to rectify my existence. The most profound relationship we'll ever have is the one with ourselves.

–Shirley MacLaine

Whenever you want to marry someone, go have lunch with his ex-wife.

–Shelley Winters

Husbands are chiefly good lovers when they are betraying their wives.

–Marilyn Monroe

No wedding bells for me anymore. I've been happily married to my profession for years.

–Shirley Bassey

I love being married. It's so great to find that one special person you want to annoy for the rest of your life.

−**Rita Rudner**

The trouble with some woman is they get all excited about nothing—and then they marry him.

−**Cher**

I am a marvelous housekeeper. Every time I leave a man I keep his house.

−**Zsa Zsa Gabor**

In our family we don't divorce our men—we bury them.

−**Ruth Gordon**

I fell off my pink cloud with a thud.

−**Elizabeth Taylor on her European honeymoon with Nicky Hilton**

If variety is the spice of life, marriage is the big can of leftover Spam.

−**Johnny Carson**

Women might be able to fake orgasms. But men can fake whole relationships.

−**Sharon Stone**

But men and women, getting along, it's a joke. We have completely different brains, it's a completely different thing.

−**Christina Applegate**

We just knew we were going to get married. We got together in Mexico City and that was it. We both phoned the people we were having affairs with at the time and said, 'You'll never believe it, I've fallen in love."

—Ringo Starr

In this movie *[X-Men]* the women are so strong and sexy! We really kick some male butt!

—Halle Berry

Sometimes it's Britney Spears, and sometimes it's Carrie Fisher. I can't tell if I have a Lolita Complex or an Oedipus Complex.

—Ben Affleck

I've had it. I want to be a full-time wife.

—Susan Hayward

God knows I love Clark, but he's the worst lay in town.

—Carole Lombard

I guess I'll just have to practice some more.

—Clark Gable

So that ends my first experience with matrimony, which I always thought a highly overrated performance.

—Isadora Duncan

The best thing about being a bachelor is that you can get into bed from either side.

—James Dean

I like when a guy makes me feel like a woman and a little girl at the same time.

−Tara Reid

Give me golf clubs, fresh air, and a beautiful partner and you can keep my golf clubs and the fresh air.

−Jack Benny

Justin [Timberlake] is everything, and what more could you want in a person? He's funny. He's cute. He's great. He just understands. I get him and he gets me, and that's cool.

−Britney Spears

Now wouldn't you think that with a new, shiny, expensive open car, and an open-neck shirt, with a pipe in my mouth to create a carefully composed study of nonchalance, sportiveness, *savoir-faire* and sophistication, I would cut quite a swath amongst ladies? Wouldn't you? *Wouldn't* you? Nothing of the sort.

−Cary Grant

Assumptions are the termites of relationships.

−Henry Winkler

I hate the whole reluctant sex-symbol thing. It's such bull ----. You see these dudes greased up, in their underwear, talking about how they don't want to be a sex symbol.

−Ben Affleck

The best smell in the world is that man that you love.
– **Jennifer Aniston**

I think I have a love for TV hosts. I can't help it. Ted Koppel was my first crush when I was three. Then I was in love with David Letterman. He's my sweetheart. But now I've got my Tom.
– **Drew Barrymore**

I really want to love somebody. I do. I just don't know if it's possible forever and ever.
– **Jim Carrey**

When David [Arquette] and I got engaged we started therapy together. I'd heard that the first year of marriage is the hardest, so we decided to work through all that stuff early.
– **Courtney Cox**

I'm not one of those fellows that is just going to have a pseudo-middling relationship.
– **Russell Crowe**

Everything I buy is vintage and smells funny. Maybe that's why I don't have a boyfriend.
– **Lucy Liu**

I think we're in a time when everyone's afraid to have sex. But I was raised with it being beautiful and healthy.
– **Alyssa Milano**

I know that he [Matthew Broderick] doesn't have his laundry done, and that he hasn't had a hot meal in days. That stuff weighs on my mind.
— Sarah Jessica Parker

When I go out with the ladies, I don't force them to try to pronounce my name. I tell them I like to go by the nickname Kitten.
— Joaquin Phoenix

I know this sounds ridiculous, but I like guys with love handles. I hate a washboard stomach—that does not turn me on.
— Tara Reid

Doing love scenes is always awkward. I mean, it's just not a normal thing to go to work and lay in bed with your co-worker.
— Denise Richards

I've never attempted to figure that out, but if you want me to take a wild guess, I'll say 5,000."
— Charlie Sheen on how many women he's slept with

I don't have a boyfriend right now. I'm looking for anyone with a job that I don't have to support.
— Anna Nicole Smith

I've been with a beautiful girl from time to time.
— David Spade

When you're comfortable with someone you love, the silence is the best.
– Britney Spears

I haven't been with a woman in nine months.
– Mike Tyson

I've dated the sweet mama's boy, the musician rocker, the struggling artist–basically a lot of people without jobs.
– Alyssa Milano

If only I could find a guy who wasn't in his 70s to talk to me about white cranes, I'd be madly in love.
– Leelee Sobieski

People say, "He [husband Guy Ritchie] turned my head." My head spun around on my body!
– Madonna

I haven't had sex in eight months. To be honest, I now prefer to go bowling.
– Lil' Kim

Rumors about me? Calista Flockhart, Pam Anderson, and Matt Damon. That's who I'm dating.
– Ben Affleck

It was a great kiss. It even had a saliva trail.
– Sarah Michelle Gellar on her kiss with Selma Blair in *Cruel Intentions*

A girl came up to me in a bar and said she wanted to be my apple pie. I wish I'd said something cool, but I was stunned.

—Jason Biggs

I don't know why age is always an issue! Love is love plain and simple. Age has nothing to do with it.

—Catherine Zeta-Jones

Nice girls made me really nervous, claustrophobic. But broken women, women in pain, woman looking to be fixed—ah, for those women the doctor was in.

—Kelsey Grammer

You know, I feel sexier than I've ever felt in my life, because I'm free, and I'm in love, and I'm sexually satisfied. I didn't really understand what sexy was a few years ago. Now Billy has really helped me to discover what it really is to feel like a woman.

—Angelina Jolie

You may marry the man of your dreams, ladies, but fourteen years later you're married to a couch that burps.

—Roseanne Barr

Men are my hobby, if I ever got married I'd have to give it up.

—Mae West

I think that everyone should get married at least once, so you can see what a silly, outdated institution it is.

—Madonna

Sexiness wears thin after a while and beauty fades, but to be married to a man who makes you laugh every day, ah, now that's a real treat.

– Joanne Woodward

Why fool around with hamburger when you have steak at home?

– Paul Newman

I'd marry again if I found a man who had fifteen million dollars, would sign over half to me, and guarantee that he'd be dead within a year.

– Bette Davis

Father Knows Best

and other dubious facts about family life

☆ ☆ ☆ ☆ ☆ ☆ ☆ ☆

I grew up with six brothers. That's how I learned to dance—waiting for the bathroom.

–Bob Hope

I've got cousins galore. Mexicans just spread all their seeds. And the women just pop them out.

–Christine Aguilera

Happiness is having a large, loving, caring, close-knit family in another city.

–George Burns

I know that I could really kill for my daughter. I know because I'm living for her, so I'm fierce when it comes down to it. And I feel the same about my husband and my family. I'm just fiercely protective. It's like, that's my lair and nobody messes with my lair.

–Whitney Houston

I'm lucky enough to have a couple of special friendships in my life...One is my younger brother, Casey. He was in *To Die For* and *Good Will Hunting*... We're very close. I'm very, very close with my mom, whom I think is just a saint. She's a superwoman.

—Ben Affleck

Insanity runs in my family. It practically gallops.

—Cary Grant

I am the person most qualified to host a talk show. I have five kids from three different marriages; my sister and brother are both gay; I have multiple personalities; and the *National Enquirer* reunited me with my daughter.

—Roseanne Barr

We make stands in our house. My daughter is a vegan, a Buddhist, and she won't wear a leather item anywhere on her body. There are things we do all over the place that, somehow, give the message to our children that you can make a difference and make conscious choices. No toy guns in our house, that kind of thing.

—Jamie Lee Curtis

I really don't have any family, what I care about most are my friends.

—Drew Barrymore

I'm everybody's fan, because I truly respect and love the music industry and the people in it...we are a "family" and a family with a lot of potential to do good for the world around us.

—Brenda Lee

My mother always says, "I'd rather see you naked than dead."

—**Julianne Moore**

If evolution really works, how come mothers only have two hands?

—**Milton Berle**

There's no way that moving in with your parents is a sign that your life is on track.

—**Jerry Seinfeld**

I thought she'd [my mother] offer me sympathy. Instead, she said, "Don't you ever call me crying again! You wanted to be in this business, so you better toughen up!"

—**Jennifer Lopez**

You have a wonderful child. Then, when he's thirteen, gremlins carry him away and leave in his place a stranger who gives you not a moment's peace.

—**Jill Eichenberry**

If you have never been hated by your child, you have never been a parent.

—**Bette Davis**

Love and respect are the most important aspects of parenting, and of all relationships.

—**Jodie Foster**

Ask [my brother] Harpo how much he's made and that's how much I've lost.

−Chico Marx

I think that's how it is when you're young and raising a child. You feel overwhelmed, like a wave of responsibility is engulfing you, and there's a loss of self.

−Sally Field

Parents are not quite interested in justice, they are interested in quiet.

−Bill Cosby

[My mother] saw to it I was exposed to a lot of things. She couldn't afford [life's finer things], but she was very intelligent. She is basically responsible for my success.

−Denzel Washington

My dad's probably one of the kindest people in the world. When I was younger that's not how I was−I was a little spoiled brat.

−Leonardo DiCaprio

My father said to me, "never do a job that can be replaced by machines." So I thought being an actor was a job that can't be replaced by machines. But it looks as though we might be getting to that stage.

−Michael Caine

My father basically taught me, showed me how a man treats a lady. I don't know if that's extraordinary or not. To me it's standard. My father demanded a certain amount of respect, and he gave it.

−Whitney Houston

My family was musical. Everyone sang and played. Only when I was a teenager did I discover that everybody didn't do that.

−Linda Ronstadt

Oh, God, it's so hard for me and my father to understand each other. I mean, his favorite female artist is Celine Dion.

−Madonna

I don't mind looking into the mirror and seeing my father.

−Michael Douglas

My brother Fred was always very, very good. He never did anything wrong—he was too much to bear. I was always in trouble, a real pain I the ass. I suppose I wasn't much fun to be around.

−Lucille Ball

My brother, Benjamin, was born on October 6, 1953, so we are only a year and eleven days apart. My father and his younger brother, Richard, had a similar separation in age, and similar problems: in both cases the older one usually got the first crack at everything and was often preferred.

−Christopher Reeve

My brother Russell, however, understood me well. He understood that I had great moves in bed, where the two of us constantly fought for control of one small mattress. Night after night in the darkness of our bedroom, we were opponents in pajamas. Although I was six years older than Russell, I managed to be just as immature.

–Bill Cosby

She's [my mother] mainly interested in basic things like eating and breathing. She's a very secure person, sort of like, uh, normal.

–Barbra Streisand

My dad used to tell me, "You know, you got to get a haircut," and I'd say, "What is the matter with that old man. Doesn't he know how cool I look?" But looking back at the prom pictures, I feel bad for every girl.

–Adam Sandler

It was no great tragedy being Judy Garland's daughter. I had tremendously interesting childhood years—except they had little to do with being a child.

–Liza Minnelli

I'm not particularly pre-occupied with the husband/baby thing. Besides I have a dog.

–Calista Flockhart

Contraceptives should be used on every conceivable occasion.

–Spike Mulligan

Giving birth is like taking your lower lip and forcing it over your head.

−Carol Burnett

To me, life is tough enough without having someone kick you from the inside.

−Rita Rudner

I'm not interested in being Wonder Woman in the delivery room. Give me drugs.

−Madonna

There's a lot more to being a woman than being a mother, but there's a hell of a lot more to being a mother than most people suspect.

−Roseanne Barr

Brothers don't necessarily have to say anything to each other−they can sit in a room and be together and just be completely comfortable with each other.

−Leonardo DiCaprio

My parents named me Jude for two reasons−Thomas Hardy's *Jude the* Obscure and the Beatles' song, "Hey, Jude." I'm glad it was a good song. Otherwise, it would be an awful mantle to carry.

−Jude Law

After doing *One Fine Day* and playing a pediatrician on *ER*, I'll never have kids. I'm going to have a vasectomy.

−George Clooney

[My daughters and I] have a deal where they're not allowed to have sex until after I'm dead.

–Billy Crystal

Having a child is surely the most beautifully irrational act that two people in love can commit.

–Bill Cosby

Raising kids is party joy and part guerilla warfare.

–Ed Asner

The biggest lesson we have to give our children is truth.

–Goldie Hawn

Never raise your hands to your kids. It leaves your groin unprotected.

–Red Buttons

One of the things I've discovered in general about raising kids is that they really don't give a damn if you walked five miles to school. They want to deal with what's happening now.

–Patty Duke

I ask people why they have deer heads on their walls, and they say, "Because it's such a beautiful animal." There you go. Well, I think my mother's attractive, but I have photographs of her.

–Ellen DeGeneres

It's a family that's loaded with grudges and passion. We come from a long line of robbers and highwaymen in Italy, you know. Killers, even.

– **Nicolas Cage**

Family is a mixed blessing. You're glad to have one, but it's also like receiving a sentence for a crime you didn't commit.

– **Richard Pryor**

I never met a kid I liked.

– **W.C. Fields**

I didn't realize the impact that my relationship with my grandfather had on my life until much later. He's not around anymore. He passed away when I was 11. But he taught me all the principles of how I run my life. He was a very spiritual person. He taught me how to meditate, and he always said I wasn't an extension of anybody else or the town I lived in. He said I had a new life to do whatever I want with and to be a good person and to just take opportunities as they come and go, with the flow, day by day.

– **Pamela Anderson**

Parents just don't understand.

– **Will Smith**

I have these slumber parties with my father (Aerosmith's Steve Tyler), and when we can't sleep we stay up all night trading beauty tips. He knows all about the good creams and masks.

– **Liv Tyler**

Today at eight-six my mother is well, very active, wiry and witty, and extremely good company. Sometimes we laugh together until tears come into our eyes. She is a small woman, and looking at her, I often puzzle how I grew to be 6'2".

—Cary Grant

Normally mothers-in-law have a little cat or a doggie. No, she has 72 lions, an elephant, and a bunch of snakes. Oh, boy!

—Antonio Banderas

I learned early on that family, as far as my mother and father, were not an option.

—Drew Barrymore

Family is my main priority. Shelby, my son, is three years old. Need I say more? He's quite a character and he keeps us thoroughly entertained, he's the entertainer of the family.

—Reba McEntire

[My daughter Lourdes and I] listen to Britney Spears songs together.

—Madonna

We're just going to do the best we can [with our children], hold our breath and hope we've set enough money aside for their therapy.

—Michelle Pfeiffer

My family is like a sanctuary to me. I always turn to them for support and strength. I take comfort in knowing no matter which path I choose, my family stands behind me.

—Benjamin Bratt

I'm a mother with two small children, so I don't take as much crap as I used to.

—Pamela Anderson

Other mothers help me with chauffeuring the kids around, and I do the same for them. I believe that in order to do all we need to, we need help, and I've found that others are willing to form a network with you.

—Maria Shriver

My daughter made me a Jerry Springer-watching kit, with crackers, Cheez Whiz, polyester stretch pants and a T-shirt with two fat women fighting over a skinny guy.

—Roseanne Barr

I'm so much more than just Angelina [Jolie's] brother. I'm also Jon Voight's son and Billy Bob Thorton's brother-in-law.

—James Haven

Even just on a selfish level...[kids] enrich you. But it's the hardest thing in the world, especially for someone who is independent.

—Lisa Kudrow

I know for me, a lot of my 20s was about going off and proving that I wasn't like my mother [Frederica Brenneman, a

Superior Court judge in Connecticut]. I was so different, I wasn't going to do anything like her. And then, we all know, you fall flat on your face, because you're exactly like your parents.

–Amy Brenneman

[As the only brother of three sisters], no woman in this world puts fear in me at all. I feel totally relaxed, I don't care if it's the Queen of England or a hooker on the street.

–Liam Neeson

The easiest way to convince my kids that they don't really need something is to get it for them.

–Joan Collins

I work with kids all day. Every day. And a lot of the night. It's not something I'm not used to. Only these kids listen to me which is different from my own. That's interesting too. I'd go, "OK, everybody be quiet." And they'd be quiet. I could do that for hours [at home] and it's like my voice doesn't exist.

–Meryl Streep

You see much more of your children once they leave home.

–Lucille Ball

When a child abruptly quadruples her family's income, some changes may be expected.

–Shirley Temple

My earliest memories include Saturday afternoon walks with Daddy over to Central Avenue, where many of the black entertainers performed and had offices. Mama would doll me up—my nickname was always Dolly—and Daddy would take me out for his special time with him. But we weren't looking for Lena Horne. Daddy took me to the barber and the grocer and the cleaners: This is my Doll," he would say, showing me off.

—Darlene Love

Music is an outgrowth of family—and my family comes first.

—Bob Dylan

I've had a child in the house since February of 1968, and let me tell you something...I've kind of had it! This is the first time I've ever not had the responsibility, on a daily basis, of having to watch the kids.

—Michelle Phillips

My kids looked as though they were twenty years older. In six weeks they had changed enough for me to feel resentful that I had missed out on some vital part of their development, and I made up my mind never to spend any time away from home unless I could take them with me.

—Gene Kelly

I cry in movie theatres all the time. I get that from my grandfather. We're really a sentimental family.

—Backstreet Boy Kevin Richardson

Child acting is a cutthroat world, which is pretty frightening and really silly in retrospect. But it's the parents who are evil.... It is a really difficult world to live in if you don't have a base, if you don't have a strong sense of yourself. My mom wanted me to maintain a reasonable degree of normalcy and to enjoy my childhood.

−Elijah Woods

And then, having two children. Without any question, it's made me a better actor and a better person.

−Rob Lowe

My [daughter] Antonia is stubborn and bending, trusting and suspicious, touch as bricks and soft as down. She is resolute. She is whatever she needs to be to survive, and to drag me with her into the next century. She is every child I ever had, every woman I ever loved, every picture I ever made. She is my past, present, and future.

−Anthony Quinn

I had the perfect younger sister-older brother relationship with Karen. Sure, there were times when I though it was an imposition that she would always have to come with me, and that I had to stick up for her, fight for her, and defend her. Mostly though, I was proud to be responsible for her. If I saw somebody hurt my sister, I was going to hurt him.

−Kelsey Grammer

Some parents get better children than they deserve.

−Raymond Burr

A child of one can be taught not to do certain things such as touch a hot stove, turn on the gas, pull lamps off their tables by their cords, or wake Mommy before noon.

—Joan Rivers

I figure that if the children are alive when I get home, I've done my job.

—Roseanne Barr

The Color of Money

to have and have not

☆ ☆ ☆ ☆ ☆ ☆ ☆ ☆

I don't have any use for bodyguards, but I do have a specific use for two highly trained certified public accountants.
–Elvis Presley

I want only two houses, rather than seven....I feel like letting go of things.
–Barbra Streisand

I'm staggered by the question of what it's like to be a multi-millionaire. I always have to remind myself that I am.
–Bruce Willis

My doctor gave me six months to live, but when I couldn't pay the bill, he gave me six months more.
–Walter Matthau

Money is of value for what it buys, and in love it buys time, place, intimacy, comfort, and a private corner alone.
–Mae West

A bank is a place that will lend you money if you can prove that you don't need it.

–Bob Hope

I enjoy money. Not enough people in this world are happy. I'm determined to be contented, and having plenty of money from working makes it easier for me.

–Karen Carpenter

When you're as rich as I am, you don't have to be political.

–Sting

This film cost $31 million. With that kind of money I could have invaded some country.

–Clint Eastwood

I have enough money to last me the rest of my life, unless I buy something.

–Jackie Mason

I am not making as much money as I thought I would. There so much money in the world, I figure at least twenty billion of it belongs to me.

–Denzel Washington

Money doesn't talk, it swears.

–Bob Dylan

The poor speak very fast, with quick movements, to attract attention. The rich move slowly and they speak slowly;

they don't need to get your attention because they've already got it.

—Michael Caine

Don't let your mouth write no check that your tail can't cash.

—Bo Diddley

My boyfriend keeps telling me I've got to own things. So, first I bought this car. And then he told me I oughta get a house. "Why a house?" "Well, you gotta have a place to park the car."

—Julia Roberts

I don't care if people think I'm a dumb blonde or stupid or an overage actress or over the hill. I'm gonna have a very successful Internet company, and I'm gonna have 100 million in the bank and I don't give a sh-- what anybody thinks.

—Melanie Griffith

Some rock musicians make a bunch of money and stick it up their noses—I stick mine in my ear.

—Frank Zappa

That's the trouble with being me. At this point, nobody gives a damn what my problem is. I could literally have a tumor on the side of my head and they'd be like, "Yeah, Big deal. I'd eat a tumor every morning for the kinda money you're pulling down."

—Jim Carrey

I don't want anything I don't deserve, [but] if they offer me more money, I'm not a-stupid.
— **Antonio Banderas**

I want a man who's kind and understanding. Is that too much to ask of a millionaire?
— **Zsa Zsa Gabor**

Most people work just hard enough not to get fired and get paid just enough money not to quit.
— **George Carlin**

I've got all the money I'll ever need if I die by four o'clock.
— **Henny Youngman**

A thing worth having is a thing worth cheating for.
— **W.C. Fields**

I enjoy being a highly overpaid actor.
— **Roger Moore**

If you build up a business big enough, it's respectable.
— **Will Rogers**

People ask why you need anything larger than twenty-two rooms. You don't need any more than a living room, kitchen, bedroom, and bath. But what you want is something else again.
— **Cher**

The only reason I'm in Hollywood is that I don't have the moral courage to refuse the money.

—Marlon Brando

I'd like to be rich enough so that I could throw soap away after the letters are worn off.

—Andy Rooney

No gold-digging for me...I take diamonds! We may be off the gold standard someday.

—Mae West

I like men who are prematurely wealthy.

—Joan Rivers

It isn't necessary to be rich and famous to be happy. It is only necessary to be rich.

—Alan Alda

I've been in trouble all my life; I've done the most unutterable rubbish, all because of money. I didn't need it...the lure of the zeroes was simply too great.

—Richard Burton

A diamond is the only kind of ice that keeps a girl warm.

—Elizabeth Taylor

I don't want to make money. I just want to be wonderful.

—Marilyn Monroe

Sharing money is what gives it its value.

—Elvis Presley

Some people get so rich they lose all respect for humanity. That's how rich I want to be.

−**Rita Rudner**

Money can't buy friends, but you can get a better class of enemy.

−**Spike Mulligan**

It is easy to be independent when you've got money. But to be independent when you haven't got a thing, that's the Lord's test.

−**Mahalia Jackson**

You have no idea how much it costs to make a person look this cheap.

−**Dolly Parton**

I'm proud to be paying taxes in the United States. The only thing is—I could be just as proud for half the money.

−**Arthur Godfrey**

You don't see me at Vegas or at the races throwing my money around. I've got a government to support.

−**Bob Hope**

I've never sought success in order to get fame and money; it's the talent and the passion that count in success.

−**Ingrid Bergman**

Money is better than poverty, if only for financial reasons.

−**Woody Allen**

Bankruptcy is a legal proceeding in which you put your money in your pants pocket and give your coat to your creditors.

– Joey Adams

Why is there so much month left at the end of the money?

– John Barrymore

I was once so poor I didn't know where my next husband was coming from.

– Mae West

My problem lies in reconciling my gross habits with my net income.

– Errol Flynn

A study of economics usually reveals that the best time to buy anything is last year.

– Marty Allen

I've been rich and I've been poor; rich is better.

– Sophie Tucker

Money can't buy happiness, but it will certainly get you a better class of memories.

– Ronald Reagan

The only thing money gives you is the freedom of not worrying about money.

– Johnny Carson

There were times when my pants were so thin that I could sit on a dime and tell if it were heads or tails.
–**Spencer Tracy**

I had to sell my saucepan so I could buy something to cook in it.
–**Woody Guthrie**

There's only one thing money won't buy, and that is poverty.
–**Joe E. Lewis**

Poor people have more fun than rich people, they say; but I notice it's the rich people who keep saying it.
–**Jack Paar**

Money will not make you happy, and happy will not make you money.
–**Groucho Marx**

A man that hoards up riches and enjoys them not, is like an ass that carries gold and eats thistles.
–**Richard Burton**

Any man who has $10,000 left when he dies is a failure.
–**Errol Flynn**

Habitually, I'm a man who examines and totals the restaurant check. And so should you at today's prices; but if you're afraid to, disinclined to, or too embarrassed to, then that's up to you. I indulge in no such insecurities. I examine my bills.

Just as any other sensible man would when doing business at any other place.

—Cary Grant

I am going to be pretty kick a$$ by the time I'm thirty, and I can't wait!!

—Rose McGowan

I bought my momma everything she wanted. But, you know, stuff changes when you start making money, because your momma treats you different... She don't fuss at you no more. You know, if I leave a plate on the table, she'd be like, "Who left this plate on the table?" I said, "I did, Momma." She'd say, "Oh, that's OK, baby. I wanted the plate right there on the table. Look at that plate, that plate looks so good right there. I just came up with a great idea just because you left that plate on the table. Would you buy me another car, baby?"

—Chris Tucker

You know, you can do some things just because you have more money than you used to have. So those kinds of things change, but fortunately, everything else stays the same.

—Goran Visnjic

I think I'm making money; I know I'm spending a hell of a lot! I'm able to do things I've always wanted to do...I'm going to Alaska to fish for pleasure, I bought my mother her first new car, I've bought land to building a house on...

—Mark Chestnutt

I'm not into the money thing. You can only sleep in one bed at a time. You can only eat one meal at a time, or be in one car at a time. So I don't have to have millions of dollars to be happy. All I need are clothes on my back, a decent meal, and a little loving when I feel like it. That's the bottom line.

—Ray Charles

I can't stand to see red in my profit-or-loss column. I'm Taurus the bull, so I react to red. If I see it, I sell my stocks quickly.

—Barbra Streisand

No money, no material reward is comparable to the praise, the shouts of well done and accompanying pat on the back of one's fellowman.

—Cary Grant

You know you've entered a new territory when you realize that your dress cost more than your film.

—Jessica Yu

I work hard. I think, "It's about time, dammit!" So it's fun, especially when you know that you delivered. The first movie [*Rush Hour*] made close to $300 million. If the movie wouldn't have done that, then it wouldn't have made that much sense to pay me that much. But it really ain't a lot of money when you look at it.

—Chris Tucker

Send me whatever you want, I'll wear it. I'm an idiot—I should talk about Tiffany's. Let me give a plug to the Federal Reserve. My favorite bill is the one hundred.

—David Duchovny

I don't think it's a joke that people put up $20 million to finance a movie. I show up. I know my lines.

−Reese Witherspoon

They say I left a train of broken hearts behind me when I left California for New York. Now I wouldn't do a thing like that. The fact is I left a trail of broken bottles and unpaid bills.

−Bing Crosby

Hollywood was once an El Dorado where almost everyone was making enormous sums of money. Staying in touch with reality often wasn't easy in tinsel town.

−Tony Randall

If you compromise your independence for any reason, there's not much use for living. If you compromise it for something as fleeting as money you are already dead...

−Sean Connery

I was just going crazy doing that type of work. I was earning a ton of money, before Zeppelin. They all though I was crazy for giving it up....I was becoming a vegetable. I wasn't saying anything musically. I was churning this stuff out and, as I said, making a ton of money, doing 20-30 arrangements a month, for everybody.

−John Paul Jones

I consider myself a fortunate man because I have always been paid so well for something I would gladly do for nothing. My profession is my hobby and recreation as well.

−Tony Randall

It doesn't make me a better actor or make me work harder or less hard. I'm as on time to work now as when I got paid scale-plus-ten. Nothing changes because of how much you get paid except how much you get paid. And the fact that people ask you about how much you get paid, which, where I grew up, wasn't an appropriate question to ask somebody.

—Julia Roberts

I *like* money. Anybody know anyone who doesn't? You *do?* He's a liar.

—Cary Grant

Young at Heart

but what about all the other parts?

☆ ☆ ☆ ☆ ☆ ☆ ☆ ☆

I have everything I had twenty years ago, only it's all a little lower.

–Gypsy Rose Lee

The secret of staying young is to live honestly, eat slowly, and lie about your age.

–Lucille Ball

My worst fear is that I'll end up living in some run-down duplex on Wilshire wearing pants hiked up to my nipples and muttering under my breath.

–Richard Dreyfuss

Old people don't need companionship. They need to be isolated and studied so it can be determined what nutrients they have that might be extracted for our personal use.

–Homer Simpson

Middle age is when you're faced with two temptations, and you choose the one that will get you home by nine o'clock.

–Ronald Reagan

People have this obsession. They want you to be like you were in 1969. They want you to, because otherwise their youth goes with you.

–Mick Jagger

There are only three ages for women in Hollywood—Babe, District Attorney, and Driving Miss Daisy.

–Goldie Hawn

It is very tough for me, getting older—and, of course, everything slows down. But I think I had really good training when I was young, which is why I can still do a lot of things. And another good thing is that I decide on how the fighting scenes will go—I know what I can and can't do.

–Jackie Chan

I'm at an age where my back goes out more than I do.

–Phyllis Diller

It really costs me a lot emotionally to watch myself on-screen. I think of myself, and feel like I'm quite young, and then I look at this old man with the baggy chins and the tired eyes and the receding hairline and all that.

–Gene Hackman

You're only young once, but you can always be immature.

–Dave Barry

I'm now at an age where I've got to prove I'm just as good as I never was.

–Rex Harrison

Gray hair is God's graffiti.

–Bill Cosby

You don't get older, you get better.

–Shirley Bassey

By the time you're eighty years old you've learned everything. You only have to remember it.

–George Burns

I think in twenty years I'll be looked at like Bob Hope. Doing those president jokes and golf shit. It scares me.

–Eddie Murphy

I'm quite comfortable with the reality of my age, and I don't feel old. I'll continue to do physical roles until it begins to hurt too much.

–Harrison Ford

I never thought I'd be sixty. It's not that I didn't expect to live this long. It's just that—well, sixty! That's almost old. I was afraid that by the time I reached fifty I wouldn't be myself anymore. I guess that when you spend your life as a dancer and an actor you learn to view the passing of time like the ticking of a time bomb: five more years until annihilation...four more years until annihilation...thirty minutes until annihilation

–Valerie Harper

The age I'm at now, you go from being a young girl to suddenly you blossom into a woman. You ripen, you know? And then you start to rot.

−Liv Tyler

You have to stay in shape. My grandmother, she started walking five miles a day when she was 60. She's 97 today and we don't know where the hell she is.

−Ellen DeGeneres

Keep on raging−to stop the aging.

−The Delltones

At twenty you have many desires which hide the truth, but beyond forty there are only real and fragile truths−your abilities and your failings.

−Gerard Depardieu

You can't be as old as I am without waking up with a surprised look on your face every morning: "Holy Christ, whaddya know - I'm still around!" It's absolutely amazing that I survived all the booze and smoking and the cars and the career.

−Paul Newman

Careful grooming may take 20 years off a woman's age, but you can't fool a long flight of stairs.

−Marlene Dietrich

I won't say I'm out of condition now−but I even puff going downstairs.

−Dick Gregory

I might be just twenty-six, but I'm an old woman in disguise ... twenty-six goin' on sixty-five.

—Aretha Franklin

There is a fountain of youth: it is your mind, your talents, the creativity you bring to your life and the lives of the people you love. When you learn to tap this source, you will truly have defeated age.

—Sophia Loren

To me, life is like the back nine in golf. Sometimes you play better on the back nine. You may not be stronger, but hopefully you're wiser. And if you keep most of your marbles intact, you can add a note of wisdom to the coming generation.

—Clint Eastwood

Most producers do prefer a 27-year-old to a 41-year-old...I'm stupid that I gave [my age] away when I was a kid! That's the thing I've realized the most in the last few years.

—Melanie Griffith

No matter how old you get, if you can keep the desire to be creative, you're keeping the man-child alive.

—John Cassavetes

From birth to age 18, a girl needs good parents, from 18 to 35 she needs good looks, from 35 to 55 she needs a good personality, and from 55 on she needs cash.

—Sophie Tucker

The hardest years in life are those between ten and seventy.

—Helen Hayes

The four stages of man are infancy, childhood, adolescence, and obsolescence.

— **Art Linkletter**

Sometimes I feel like an old hooker.

— **Cher**

Middle age is when your age starts to show around the middle.

— **Bob Hope**

Old age is when the liver spots show through your gloves.

— **Phyllis Diller**

You can lie back and become elderly or you can hitch up your jeans and go forward.

— **Elizabeth Taylor**

I want to grow old without face-lifts...I want to have the courage to be loyal to the face I have made. Sometimes I think it would be easier to avoid old age, to die young, but then you'd never complete you life, would you? You'd never wholly know yourself.

— **Marilyn Monroe**

I don't think you should try to hide your experience. My role model is Jessica Tandy, who was working while she was in her 80s. So 50 doesn't strike terror, for me.

— **Sigourney Weaver**

When I'm 33 I'll quit. That's the time when a man has to do something else. I can't say what it'll definitely be...but it won't be in show business. I couldn't bear to end up as an Elvis Presley and sing in Las Vegas with all the housewives and old ladies coming in with their handbags. It's really sick.

—**Mick Jagger**

Women are not forgiven for aging. Robert Redford's lines of distinction are my old age wrinkles.

—**Jane Fonda**

It is sad to grow old but nice to ripen.

—**Brigitte Bardot**

If you survive long enough, you're revered—rather like an old building.

—**Katharine Hepburn**

Age is a very high price to pay for maturity.

—**Tom Stoppard**

I'll be dead by the time I'm forty.

—**Rod Stewart**

Nice to be here? At my age it's nice to be anywhere.

—**George Burns**

The older you get, the stronger the wind gets—and it's always in your face.

—**Jack Nicholson**

It is sobering to consider that when Mozart was my age he had already been dead for a year.

−Tom Lehrer

One thing about being successful is that I stopped being afraid of dying. Once you're a star you're dead already. You're embalmed.

−Dustin Hoffman

Old age is like everything else. To make a success of it, you've got to start young.

−Fred Astaire

Age is not important unless you're a cheese.

−Helen Hayes

I hope I never get so old I get religious.

−Ingmar Bergman

After thirty, a body has a mind of its own.

−Bette Midler

Old age ain't no place for sissies.

−Bette Davis

The really frightening thing about middle age is the knowledge that you'll grow out of it.

−Doris Day

I've been around so long I knew Doris Day before she was a virgin.
–**Groucho Marx**

I was born in 1962. True. And the room next to me was 1963.
–**Joan Rivers**

I believe in loyalty. When a woman reaches a certain age she likes, she should stick with it.
–**Eva Gabor**

We decided not to light the candles this year: we were afraid Pan Am would mistake it for a runway.
–**Bob Hope**

Now that I'm over sixty, I'm veering toward respectability.
–**Shelley Winters**

I am very attractive and get cuter the older I get. I'm even getting—well, not statuesque, but I'm growing. I'm expanding. That's the best way to put it.
–**Whoopi Goldberg**

As you get older, the pickings get slimmer, but the people don't.
–**Carrie Fisher**

If I live to be a hundred, there won't be time to do everything I want.

−**James Dean**

Like, I'm nineteen. What am I supposed to do, play a judge?!

−**Winona Ryder**

It's ill-becoming from an old broad to sing about how bad she wants it. But occasionally we do.

−**Lena Horne**

I hate it. I hated my 40th. My 50th and 55th were fine, but this one, I'm just not enjoying it. I don't see it. If I don't look in the mirror I'm 24. But 60 – I have all those images from my child-hood. People who are 60 are just...old. Mind you, at 45 I was derelict.

−**Ringo Starr**

I do have to pinch myself to make sure I'm not dead.

−**Lauren Bacall**

I'm only two years older than Brad Pitt, but I look a lot older, which used to greatly frustrate me. It doesn't anymore. I don't have to fit into that category and get trounced by Tom Cruise and Brad.

−**George Clooney**

That's what being young is all about. You have the courage and the daring to think that you can make a difference. You're not prone to measure your energies in time. You're not likely to live by equations.

−**Ruby Dee**

Retirement: I prefer to leave standing up, like a well-mannered guest at a party.
—**Leontyne Price**

It's hard for me to get used to these changing times. I can remember when the air was clean and sex was dirty.
—**George Burns**

The only parts left of my original body are my elbows.
—**Phyllis Diller**

No! Never! I will never retire. Death before dishonor!
—**Ed Asner**

I look fabulous for my age.
—**Jane Fonda**

I cried on my 18th birthday. I thought 17 was such a nice age. You're young enough to get away with things, but you're old enough, too.
—**Liv Tyler**

I've honestly not been too aware of my age until I went to the doctor for a full check-up. He said I had the heart of a young man— "but you're not young, you're 40."
—**Sean Connery**

Though I've turned 21, I don't drink. I'm an old hag now. I'm just an old fart.
—**Mena Suvari**

There are moments when I can't believe I'm as old as I am. But I feel better physically than I did 10 years ago. I don't think, Oh God, I'm missing something.

−**Madonna**

I'm very mature for my age, but I'm also innocent in a lot of ways.

−**Kirsten Dunst**

Interviewer: How do you feel when you see yourself in *Rocky* 25 years later.

Sylvester Stallone: As Bob Hope would say, how would you feel, sitting there watching your hairline recede?

I'd love to redo [*The Private Lives of Elizabeth and Essex*] one more time. I would feel more comfortable as the older queen. Since I am *an* older...queen.

−**Bette Davis**

What I look forward to is continued immaturity followed by death.

−**Dave Barry**

Sixty was the deadline. I promised myself long ago that by the time I reached that age I would have achieved all my goals. Another hit record. A Grammy award. A long run in a Broadway show. ...By the time I was sixty, I figured, I would have been in show business almost forty-five years. I knew that the Lord had blessed me with stamina and with a voice that was aging gracefully, but even I had to slow down at some point. How many more times could I sing "He's a Rebel"?

−**Darlene Love**

Retirement for me, as it does for almost anyone in show business, will come involuntarily: when I die. Of course, I'll never die.

– **Tony Randall**

Just want to say that music has no age. Most of your great composers–musicians–are elderly people, way up there in age–they will live forever. There's no such thing as on the way out. As long as you are still doing something interesting and good. You are in business as long as you are breathing. Yeah.

– **Louis Armstrong**

There has been an interminable quality surrounding every part of the progression, but now that the action is nearly over, I see that everything has moved with remarkable celerity. The time between childhood and old age was swift, the intermissions were confusing.

– **Anthony Quinn**

More than anything else, I'd like to be an old man with a good face, like Hitchcock or Picasso.

– **Sean Connery**

I love it. Tatia, who's 14 now and our first grandchild from Zak and Sarah calls me "Grandad." They tried to be modern parents and said, "Well, what do you want to be called?" I said, "I want to be called Grandad!" I love that.

– **Ringo Starr**

I will never lie about my age.

– **Penelope Cruz**

[My birthday is] December 31, my sixtieth. I'm glad to be above ground instead of underneath. I never thought I'd reach forty.

—Anthony Hopkins

Someone asked someone who was my age, "How are you?" The answer was, "Fine. If you don't ask details."

—Katharine Hepburn

Talk of the Town

what they say about each other, nasty and nice

☆ ☆ ☆ ☆ ☆ ☆ ☆ ☆

He [Elvis] can't last. I tell you flatly, he can't last.
— **Jackie Gleason**

Without Elvis, none of us could have made it.
— **Buddy Holly**

The Russians love Brook Shields because her eyebrows remind them of Leonid Brezhnev.
— **Robin Williams**

I find the language of George W. much more offensive [than rapper Eminem]
— **Madonna**

Boy George is all England needs—another queen who can't dress.
— **Joan Rivers**

Oh yeah, he's got it. He has this sort of charming vulnerability, George [Clooney], yet mixed with this outrageous mischievousness, so you never know what's going to happen next. From all my girlfriends, that seems to be the major question: "What's George Clooney like?" The second major question is, "Is he single?"

–Nicole Kidman

Burt Reynolds: He is the one the ladies like to dance with and their husbands like to drink with. He is the larger-than-life actor of our times. He is gifted, talented, naughty and nice.

–Frank Sinatra

She's okay if you like talent.

–Ethel Merman on Mary Martin

Let's just say there's not a drop of Jewish blood in him.

–Rob Reiner on Tom Cruise

To this day, Dolly is what country music is to me.

–Patty Loveless

I love his work but I couldn't warm to him [Chuck Berry] even if I was cremated next to him.

–Keith Richards

I have not been able to talk to Britney [Spears] at length since we were best friends on the Mickey Mouse Club. I miss her a lot. I think she's a really sweet girl who's really talented.

–Christina Aguilera

She [Joan Collins] looks like she combs her hair with an eggbeater.

−**Louella Parsons**

I could rip Madonna's throat out. I can sing better than she can.

−**Meryl Streep**

I'm better than Olivier.

−**Robert Duvall**

Miss United Dairies herself.

−**David Niven on Jayne Mansfield**

Dramatic art in her [Jayne Mansfield] opinion is knowing how to fill a sweater.

−**Bette Davis**

The closest thing to Roseanne Barr's singing the national anthem was my cat being neutered.

−**Johnny Carson**

I treasure every moment that I do not see her [Phyllis Diller].

−**Oscar Levant**

Buddy Holly made it OK to be square. Made it cool to be square. He was this very square looking guy. Just singing from his gut and making some great music.

−**Melissa Etheridge**

I didn't know her well, but after watching her [Judy Garland] I didn't want to know her well.

−**Joan Crawford**

She [Helen Reddy] ought to be arrested for loitering in front of an orchestra.

−**Bette Midler**

I see myself as Rhoda, not Mary Tyler Moore.

−**Rosie O'Donnell**

The key to any good relationship, on-screen and off, is communication, respect, and I guess you have to like the way the other person smells—and he [Keanu Reeves] smelled real nice.

−**Sandra Bullock**

Bob Dylan is so brilliant. To me, he makes William Shakespeare sounds like Billy Joel.

−**George Harrison**

It's a new low for actresses when you have to wonder what's between her [Sharon Stone] ears instead of her legs.

−**Katharine Hepburn**

Is Elizabeth Taylor fat? Her favorite food is seconds.

−**Joan Rivers**

Every minute this broad [Elizabeth Taylor] spends outside of bed is a waste of time.

–Michael Todd

She's [Drew Barrymore] like an apple turnover that got crushed in a grocery bag on a hot day.

–Camille Paglia

Mae West: A plumber's idea of Cleopatra.

–W. C. Fields

She [Zsa Zsa Gabor] has discovered the secret of perpetual middle age.

–Oscar Levant

Zsa Zsa Gabor has been married so many times she has rice marks on her face.

–Henny Youngman

Her [Marilyn Monroe] body has gone to her head.

–Barbara Stanwyck

She [Marilyn Monroe] has breasts of granite and a mind like a Gruyere cheese.

–Billy Wilder

You have this preconceived notion of him [Sly Stallone] as a big, tough guy, but he speaks four languages and he likes to watercolor.

–Rachael Leigh Cook

Matthew [McConaughey] looks gorgeous naked. He should be naked as much as possible until things start falling.

–Sandra Bullock

How could any woman resist George Clooney? He makes my knees go weak. Oh yes, I'd love him to play doctors and nurses in my next video.

–Britney Spears

I think Mick Jagger would be astounded and amazed if he realized to how many people he is not a sex symbol but a mother image.

–David Bowie

I could take Sean Connery in a fight…I could definitely take him.

–Harrison Ford

Brad [Pitt], poor geezer was blown up, thrown around, burned, slapped, frozen. But never a moan or a whine. Now that's what I call a real star.

–Guy Ritchie

Boy George makes me sick.

–Madonna

Rita Hayworth is *it*. I just watch her and think: *Wow!* I mean, she's so beautiful, *so* charismatic and an extraordinary dancer. She just takes your breath away as a performer.

–Nicole Kidman

For her [Greta Garbo], and her alone, I could have been a lesbian.

—**Joan Crawford**

He [John Travolta] was a very nice man and I remember I liked him very much but he was kind of in a spin-cycle a bit.

—**Stockard Channing**

I've walked down the street with some big stars, okay? I cannot walk two feet with John Travolta. People all clawing all over him.

—**Quentin Tarantino**

Of all the actors of the new generation it is Clint Eastwood who gives me the most hope. He is the best cowboy of modern cinema.

—**John Wayne**

...she's [Judy Garland] two up on me in suicide attempts, but I'm three up on her in nervous breakdowns. Or is it the other way around?

—**Oscar Levant**

I swear to God, I don't remember anything [Gwyneth Paltrow] was in. Some people get hot by association. I heard more about her and Brad Pitt than I ever heard about her work.

—**Jennifer Lopez**

Disney, of course, has the best casting. If he doesn't like an actor, he just tears him up.

—**Alfred Hitchcock**

You can sit down with the man [Robert Redford], and we'll be equals, we'll swap stories, we'll swap ideas across the table. But he's still the man! You know, I just turned into a little kid again.
—**Brad Pitt**

Marilyn Monroe: A vacuum with nipples.
—**Otto Preminger**

It was instructive to watch Clint [Eastwood] move around because he reduced everything to an absolute minimum. If he had a four-line speech, he would reduce it to four words and it was enormously effective.
—**Richard Burton**

I'd love to be a dead body in the emergency room and have George Clooney go, "This one's gone!" while he puts a sheet on me.
—**Rosie O'Donnell**

I would give anything if I could sing like you.
—**Sophia Loren to Barbra Streisand**

If I could look like you, I wouldn't even wanna talk.
—**Barbra Streisand to Sophia Loren**

I had no disagreement with Barbra Streisand. I was merely exasperated at her tendency to become a complete megalomaniac.
—**Walter Matthau**

Barbra Streisand is funny and fun—both very sexy qualities in a woman—and she has a very special beauty both without and within. It was exciting to see her creative focus, that tidal wave of creative energy and imagination.

—**Pierce Brosnan**

Joan [Crawford] always cries a lot. Her tear ducts must be close to her bladder.

—**Bette Davis**

She speaks five languages and can't act in any of them.

—**John Gielgud on Ingrid Bergman**

Who picks your clothes—Stevie Wonder?

—**Don Rickles to David Letterman**

Comparing Madonna with Marilyn Monroe is like comparing Rachel Welch to the back of a bus.

—**Boy George**

I never watch the *Dinah Shore Show*—I'm a diabetic.

—**Oscar Levant**

Hah! I always knew Frank would end up in bed with a boy!

—**Ava Gardner about Mia Farrow**

She [Bo Derek] turned down the role of Helen Keller because she couldn't remember the lines.

—**Joan Rivers**

I have more talent in my smallest fart than you have in your entire body.

–Walter Matthau to Barbra Streisand

When I look at a film of Kevin Costner's, I fall asleep out of boredom.

–Mickey Rourke

His [Mickey Rooney] favorite exercise is climbing tall people.

–Phyllis Diller

[Warren Beatty] is the type of man who will end up dying in his own arms.

–Mamie Van Doren

The only reason [Warren Beatty] had a child is so that he can meet babysitters.

–David Letterman

He [Montgomery Clift] acts like he's got a Mixmaster up his ass and doesn't want anyone to know it.

–Marlon Brando

He [John Lennon] could be a maneuvering swine, which no one ever realized.

–Paul McCartney

Goldie Hawn is funny, sexy, beautiful, talented intelligent, warm, and consistently sunny. Other than that, she doesn't impress me at all.

–Neil Simon

He [Rod Stewart] was so mean it hurt him to go to the bathroom.

–Britt Eklund

There were three things that Chico was always on–a phone, a horse, or a broad.

–Groucho Marx

Well at least he [Robert Redford] has finally found his true love...what a pity he can't marry himself.

–Frank Sinatra

He [Prince] looks like a dwarf who's been dipped in a bucket of pubic hair.

–Boy George

He [Chevy Chase] couldn't ad-lib a fart after a baked-bean dinner.

–Johnny Carson

What makes him [Clint Eastwood] think a middle-aged actor, who's played with a chimp, could have a future in politics?

–Ronald Reagan

His [Elton John] writing is limited to songs for dead blondes.

–Keith Richards

I'm glad I've given up drugs and alcohol. It would be awful to be like Keith Richards. He's pathetic. It's like a monkey with arthritis, trying to go on stage and look young. I have great respect for the Stones but they would have been better if they had thrown Keith out 15 years ago.

– Elton John

I don't even like Peter as a human being.

– Rosanna Arquette on former boyfriend Peter Gabriel

Michael Jackson's album was only called *Bad* because there wasn't room on the sleeve for the word "pathetic."

– Prince

[James] Dean died at just the right time. He left behind a legend. If he had lived, he'd never have been able to live up to his publicity.

– Humphrey Bogart

Ken is so tired his sperm are on crutches.

– Emma Thompson on ex-husband Kenneth Branagh

Julie Andrews has lilacs instead of pubic hairs.

– Christopher Plummer

Elizabeth Taylor has more chins than the Chinese telephone directory.

– Joan Rivers

Sleeping with George Michael would be like having sex with a groundhog.

– Boy George

Michael Jackson . . . he's my man. I think that he's the greatest entertainer ever because he just brings so much energy to the screen. Creatively, he took it to a whole other level.

–Chris Tucker

I think I've rarely enjoyed working with anyone as much as Johnny [Depp]. We've become friends. I really, truly found working with him a joy. He made me laugh all the time. I don't know how his image is projected, but he's really fun to be around.

–Al Pacino

Cher is a survivor. Listen, if she had been on the Titanic, they'd have cleaned off the ice and kept sailing.

–Joan Rivers

Marlon Brando: The finest actor who ever lived. He was my idol when I was 13. He's done enough work to last two lifetimes. Everything I do, I think: Can Brando play this with me?

–Barbra Streisand

Peggy Lee and Judy Garland: each of whom touches me deeply. They move me strangely, not only by their songs but by their presence. When I am with them, I feel content and happily at ease without need for oral communication.

–Cary Grant

There is not truth to the rumors that we hate each other. I have no ill feeling for Britney and vice versa. I am proud of all the achievements she has made in her career, she is a very hard working person. I have nothing, but love for her.

—Christine Aguilera

Spielberg, his great success is he's got this childlike genius. He has a great enthusiasm.

—Anthony Hopkins

In Hollywood, she's revered, she [Winona Ryder] gets nominated for Oscars, but I've never heard anyone in the public or among my friends say, "Oh, I love her."

—Jennifer Lopez

He's [Jack Nicholson] the chief, right? What else is there to say? It's not bad sleeping with Einstein.

—Lara Flynn Boyle

We talk all the time. I think we understand each other in a way that most people can't understand either of us.

—Macaulay Culkin on Michael Jackson

All those rumors about her [Calista Flockhart] being underweight are trash. She's gorgeous.

—Ben Stiller

I'm not into older guys... To tell you the truth, Richard [Gere] is not the sexiest man alive, in my book.

—Winona Ryder

People say we're all identical, but Jennifer Lopez is an American. She's from New York. She doesn't have an accent. Some of these Latin people—their Spanish is pathetic. They learned it when they became famous as Latinos.

– **Salma Hayek**

Hugh [Grant] and I both laugh and cringe at the same things, worship the same books, eat the same food, hate central heating and sleep with the window open. I thought these things were vital, but being two peas in a pod ended up not being enough.

– **Elizabeth Hurley**

He [Wesley Snipes] wouldn't talk to me for two months. I was like, "What an ass--le." Actors are used to getting their way and to treating women like objects.

– **Jennifer Lopez**

Spielberg is a good director. He's fast but flexible because he knows so much. He's so well-versed and so comfortable. He's sane! He goes home to his family at night; he loves his kids. Sometimes he'd say, "C'mon let's move! I want to get home tonight."

– **Anthony Hopkins**

Johnny [Depp] is so special that he is like a Martian. In fact, that's what I call him, Martian.

– **Penelope Cruz**

John would have been the first white rapper. And also he would have cherished the Internet.

– **Yoko Ono**

I have a sort of sisterly feeling toward him [Ben Affleck]. I want him to do well and grow up and be a happy person and a fully realized man.

– **Gwyneth Paltrow**

Martin Campbell: A wonderful director, but mad as a snake, as I am. I'm not too tightly held together either.

– **Anthony Hopkins**

Ava Gardner was the most beautiful woman in the world, and it's wonderful that she didn't cut up her face. She addressed aging by picking up her chin and receiving the light in a better way. And she looked like a woman. She never tried to look like a girl.

– **Sharon Stone**

Brad [Pitt], poor geezer, was blown up, thrown around, burned, slapped, frozen. But never a moan or a whine. Now that's what I call a real star.

– **Guy Ritchie**

I could make the whole of Manhattan disappear into that amazing butt.

– **David Copperfield on Jennifer Lopez**

Cameron Diaz: A lucky model who's been given a lot of opportunities I just wish she would have done more with.

– **Jennifer Lopez**

...the only way you can better John is by copying him exactly.

– **Yoko Ono**

The first time I met [Sylvester Stallone], he had golf tees up his nose. So I figured we were going to be OK.

–Sandra Bullock

I just want him [Tom Cruise] to wear Armani around the house and fetch me things.

–Rosie O'Donnell

Dumb and Dumber

Quips, blips, insults and more

☆ ☆ ☆ ☆ ☆ ☆ ☆ ☆

Of all the things I've ever lost, I miss my mind the most.
–Steve Tyler of Aerosmith

There's something about me that makes a lot of people want to throw up.
–Pat Boone

There's a fine line between the Method actor and the schizophrenic.
–Nicolas Cage

What is comedy? Comedy is the art of making people laugh without making them puke.
–Steve Martin

The best car safety device is a rear-view mirror with a cop in it.
–Dudley Moore

Instant gratification is not soon enough.

-Meryl Streep

Instant gratification takes too long.

-Carrie Fisher

Everybody wants to do something to help, but nobody wants to be the first.

-Pearl Bailey

Everyone hates me because I'm so popular.

-Howard Stern

I'm not an actress who can create a character. I play me.

-Mary Tyler Moore

I you stay in Beverly Hills too long you become a Mercedes.

-Robert Redford

Are there keys to a plane? Maybe that's what those delays are sometimes, when you're just sitting there at the gate. Maybe the pilot sits up there in the cockpit going, "Oh, I don't believe this. Dammit.. I did it again." They tell you it's something mechanical because they don't want to come on the P.A. system, "Ladies and gentlemen, we're going to be delayed here on the ground for a while. I uh..Oh, God this is so embarrassing... I, I left the keys to the plane in my apartment. They're in this big ashtray by the front door. I'm sorry, I'll run back and get them."

-Jerry Seinfeld

Hollywood is like Picasso's bathroom.

–Candice Bergen

I'll know my career's going badly when I start being quoted correctly.

–Lee Marvin

If you think nobody cares if you're alive, try missing a couple of car payments.

–Flip Wilson

I can hold a note as long as the Chase Manhattan Bank.

–Ethel Merman

My ancestors wandered lost in the wilderness for forty years because even in biblical times, men would not stop to ask for directions

–Elayne Boosler

Somebody once said we never know what is enough until we know what's more than enough.

–Billie Holiday

Show me a man who is content, and I'll show you a lobotomy scar.

–Sean Connery

We had gay burglars the other night. They broke in and rearranged the furniture.

–Robin Williams

Now why does moisture ruin leather? Aren't cows outside a lot of the time? When it's raining, do cows go up to the farm-house and say, "Let us in! We're all wearing leather!"?

– Jerry Seinfeld

I always wanted to be somebody, but I should have been more specific

– Lily Tomlin

I would never do crack...I would never do a drug named after a part of my own ass.

– Denis Leary

I've smoked ten marijuana cigarettes in my life. And they've given me a sore throat, a headache, and made me sleepy. I can't understand why anyone would wanna use the stuff. It seems such an impractical pastime as you can get sent to jail for it

– Frank Zappa

Therapy? I don't need that. The roles that I choose are my therapy.

– Angelina Jolie

Have you ever noticed? Anybody going slower than you is an idiot, and anyone going faster than you is a maniac.

– George Carlin

This is the first time I've had off in about 10 years. It was cool for a couple of weeks, but how much bad golf can you play?

– John Goodman

I may be the girl next door, but you wouldn't want to live next to me.

−Elizabeth Shue

Death is nature's way of killing you.

−Bill Maher

Audiences tend to love bad guys. Niceness and kindness is not rewarded as much as drama. We all try to be civil in real life, but there's a part of us that admires unequivocal evil tendencies.

−Michael Douglas

Rock 'n Roll: The most brutal, ugly, desperate, vicious form of expression it has been my misfortune to hear.

−Frank Sinatra

The only gossip I'm interested in is things from the *Weekly World News*−"Woman's bra bursts, 11 injured." That kind of thing.

−Johnny Depp

Television: A medium. So called because it's neither rare nor well done.

−Ernie Kovacs

Run for office? No. I've slept with too many women, I've done too many drugs, and I've been to too many parties.

−George Clooney

Don't do yesterday what you can't do tomorrow.

–Goldie Hawn

She not only kept her lovely figure, she's added so much to it.

–Bob Fosse

When women are depressed they either eat or go shopping. Men invade another country. It's a whole different way of thinking.

–Elayne Boosler

I am so busy doing nothing...that the idea of doing anything–which as you know always leads to something–cuts into the nothing and then forces me to have to drop everything.

–Jerry Seinfeld.

She had much in common with Hitler, only no mustache.

–Noel Coward

I come from a very long line of strong, silent types. I live by my third grade teacher's words, "Think before you stink."

–Brendan Fraser

Most rock journalism is people who can't write interviewing people who can't talk for people who can't read.

–Frank Zappa

During the next number, the ones in the cheap seats clap your hands, and the rest of you just rattle your jewelry.

–John Lennon

When I die, my epitaph should read: She Paid the Bills. That's the story of my private life.

— **Gloria Swanson**

Gone With the Wind is going to be the biggest flop in Hollywood history. I'm just glad it'll be Clark Gable who's falling flat on his face and not Gary Cooper.

— **Gary Cooper**

With two movies opening this summer, I have no relaxing time at all. Whatever I have is spent in a drunken stupor.

— **Hugh Grant**

I feel safe in white because, deep down inside, I'm an angel.

— **Sean "Puffy" Combs**

It's not that easy bein' green.

— **Kermit the Frog**

Just because you like my stuff doesn't mean I owe you anything.

— **Bob Dylan**

People will swim through shit if you put a few bob in it.

— **Peter Sellers**

Go ahead punk...Make my day...

— **Clint Eastwood**

The length of a film should be directly related to the endurance of the human bladder.
–Alfred Hitchcock

Sometimes I'm so sweet even I can't stand it.
–Julie Andrews

I wouldn't have turned out the way I was if I didn't have all those old-fashioned values to rebel against.
–Madonna

In America, through pressure of conformity, there is freedom of choice, but nothing to choose from.
–Peter Ustinov

I never believed in Santa Claus because I knew no white dude would come into my neighborhood after dark.
–Dick Gregory

I'm an old-fashioned guy.... I want to be an old man with a beer belly sitting on a porch, looking at a lake or something.
–Johnny Depp

I wasn't always black...There was this freckle, and it got bigger and bigger.
–Bill Cosby

I've been lucky enough to win an Oscar, write a best-seller—my other dream would be to have a painting in the Louvre. The only way that's going to happen is if I paint a dirty one on the wall of the gentlemen's lavatory.

–David Niven

I drive with my knees. Otherwise, how can I put on my lipstick and talk on the phone?

–Sharon Stone

I think half of this [Academy Award for *Cat Ballou*] belongs to a horse somewhere out in the valley.

–Lee Marvin

They've got great respect for the dead in Hollywood...but none for the living.

–Errol Flynn

Liberals feel unworthy of their possessions. Conservatives feel they deserve everything they've stolen.

–Mort Sahl

I don't want any yes-men around me. I want everybody to tell me the truth, even if it costs them their jobs.

–Sam Goldwyn

I cannot sing, dance or act; what else would I be but a talk show host.

–David Letterman

My only regret in the theater is that I could never sit out front and watch me.

–John Barrymore

If I play a stupid girl and ask a stupid question I've got to follow it through. What am I supposed to do—look intelligent?

–Marilyn Monroe

It's not the most intellectual job in the world, but I do have to know the letters.

–Vanna White

It is difficult to produce a television documentary that is both incisive and probing when every twelve minutes one is interrupted by twelve dancing rabbits singing about toilet paper.

–Rod Serling

Performing's like sex. You might like it but you don't wanna do it all the time.

–Mick Jagger

I never had a problem with drugs, only with cops.

–Keith Richards

As an actor, I guess I spent some of my finest moments in bed—the Gipper's death in *Knute Rockne—All American*, then a scene in *Kings Row*, in which I discovered my legs had been amputated by a sadistic and vindictive surgeon who was angry that I had romanced his daughter.

–Ronald Reagan

When did I realize I was God? Well, I was praying and I suddenly realized I was talking to myself.

–Peter O'Toole

Death is nature's way of saying, Your table's ready.
—Robin Williams

I get to go to lots of overseas places, like Canada.
—Britney Spears on fame

The cost of living is going up and the chance of living is going down.
—Flip Wilson

I never set out to be weird. It was always other people who called me weird.
—Frank Zappa

Committee—a group of men who keep minutes and waste hours.
—Milton Berle

The Supreme Court has ruled that they cannot have a nativity scene in Washington, D.C. This wasn't for any religious reasons. They couldn't find three wise men and a virgin.
—Jay Leno

It was called the Backstreet Market, and it was just like a local hangout. That was where the kids would drive their cars, hang out with their convertibles and listen to music. That's how we got "Backstreet." We put "Boys" on it, because no matter how old we get, we'll always be boys.
—Kevin Richardson

I don't mind living in a man's world as long as I can be a woman in it.

−**Marilyn Monroe**

At a formal dinner party, the person nearest death should always be seated closest to the bathroom.

−**George Carlin**

I have to go now. I'm having an old friend for dinner.

−**Anthony Hopkins in** *Silence of the Lambs*

I was planning to go into architecture [in college]. But when I arrived, architecture was filled up. Acting was right next to it, so I signed up for acting instead.

−**Tom Selleck**

Someone who makes you laugh is a comedian. Someone who makes you think and then laugh is a humorist.

−**George Burns**

I've been accused of vulgarity. I say that's bullshit.

−**Mel Brooks**

First of all, I choose the great [roles], and if none of these come, I choose the mediocre ones, and if they don't come, I choose the ones that pay the rent.

−**Michael Caine**

When you go to the mind reader, do you get half-price?

−David Letterman

Exhilaration is that feeling you get just after a great idea hits you, and just before you realize what's wrong with it.

−Rex Harrison

Why is it when we talk to God, we're praying, but when God talks to us, we're schizophrenic?

−Lily Tomlin

I've made so many movies playing a hooker that they don't pay me in the regular way anymore. They leave it on the dresser.

−Shirley MacLaine

You only lie to two people in your life: your girlfriend and the police.

−Jack Nicholson

In America you can go on the air and kid the politicians, and the politicians can go on the air and kid the people.

−Groucho Marx

She doesn't like me and I don't like her, so it's neutral.

−Sean Penn

Modesty is the artifice of actors, similar to passion in call girls.

−Jackie Gleason

Acting is the most minor of gifts and not a very high-class way to earn a living. After all, Shirley Temple could do it at the age of four.

–Katharine Hepburn

His golf bag does not contain a full set of irons.

–Robin Williams

Why are we honoring this man? Have we run out of human beings?

–Milton Berle

She should get a divorce and settle down.

–Jack Paar

I can't stand light. I hate weather. My idea of heaven is moving from one smoke-filled room to another.

–Peter O'Toole

I don't have pet peeves, I have whole kennels of irritation.

–Whoopi Goldberg

She's the kind of woman who climbed the ladder of success—wrong by wrong.

–Mae West

An intellectual snob is someone who can listen to the *William Tell Overture* and not think of *The Lone Ranger*.

–Dan Rather

What you said hurt me very much. I cried all the way to the bank.

—**Liberace**

For three days after death, hair and fingernails continue to grow but phone calls taper off.

—**Johnny Carson**

Shock is still fun. I won't ever shut the door on it.

—**Nicolas Cage**

There used to be a real me, but I had it surgically removed.

—**Peter Sellers**

I've been on a calendar, but never on time.

—**Marilyn Monroe**

Stay with me; I want to be alone.

—**Joey Adams**

Women should try to increase their size rather than decrease it, because I believe the bigger we are, the more space we'll take up, and the more we'll have to be reckoned with. I think every woman should be fat like me.

—**Roseanne Barr**

What's going to be on your tombstone?

—**"Crabby Whoopi Goldberg"**

Too much of a good thing can be wonderful.

—**Mae West**

I am just a person trapped inside a woman's body.

─Elayne Boosler

I started as a moron...and I worked up to be an imbecile in *Adam's Rib*. What I want to know is: where does a girl go from being an imbecile? Maybe if I'm lucky, I can be an idiot or a cretin.

─Judy Holliday

I used to sleep nude─until the earthquake.

─Alyssa Milano

Happiness is good health and a bad memory.

─Ingrid Bergman

Happiness? A good cigar, a good meal, a good woman─or a bad woman; it depends on how much happiness you can handle.

─George Burns

If you want to say it with flowers, remember that a single rose screams in your face: "I'm cheap!"

─Delta Burke

When a man gives his opinion he's a man. When a woman gives her opinion she's a bitch.

─Bette Davis

If it's so natural to kill, why do men have to go into training to learn how?

─Joan Baez

Today you can go to a gas station and find the cash register open and the toilets locked. They must think toilet paper is worth more than money.
—**Joey Bishop**

Do infants enjoy infancy as much as adults enjoy adultery?
—**George Carlin**

There aren't any hard women, only soft men.
—**Raquel Welch**

Americans will put up with anything provided it doesn't block traffic.
—**Dan Rather**

Acting is largely a matter of farting about in disguises.
—**Peter O'Toole**

It's not that I'm afraid to die. I just don't want to be there when it happens.
—**Woody Allen**

Some of my best leading men have been dogs and horses.
—**Elizabeth Taylor**

She got her good looks from her father. He's a plastic surgeon.
—**Groucho Marx**

When I was in second grade, we had to color the fruits their right colors, but I colored them all yellow. The teacher said,

"Don't you know that an apple is red and an orange is orange?"
I said, "Yes, but I like yellow."
–Goldie Hawn

A synonym is a word you use when you can't spell the word you first thought of.
–Burt Bacharach

Sometimes when I'm swimming, I think maybe someday, I'll put my red Speedo up for auction. Or maybe I'll donate it to the Smithsonian Museum. They can stuff it with two plums and a gherkin and put it on display.
–David Duchovny

If men can run the world, why can't they stop wearing neckties? How intelligent is it to start the day by tying a little noose around your neck?
–Linda Ellerbee

He's so small, he's a waste of skin.
–Fred Allen

I think they should have a Barbie with a buzz cut.
–Ellen DeGeneres

It was nice to go into this fake courtroom [on the *Ally McBeal* set]. I immediately went up into the judge's chair. Nice view. A preferable perspective.

–Robert Downey Jr.

Britain is the only country in the world where the food is more dangerous than the sex.

–Jackie Mason

He has Van Gogh's ear for music.

–Billy Wilder

I was the first woman to burn my bra–it took the fire department four days to put it out.

–Dolly Parton

He had a winning smile, but everything else was a loser.

–George C. Scott

The thing that separates us from the animals is our ability to accessorize.

–Olympia Dukakis in *Steel Magnolias*

If there's anything disgusting about the movie business, it's the whoredom of my peers.

–Sean Penn

I read part of it all the way through.

–Samuel Goldwyn

Her ad lib lines were well rehearsed.

–Rod Stewart

If opportunity doesn't knock, build a door.

–Milton Berle

Too bad all the people that know how to run the country are busy driving taxicabs and cutting hair.

–George Burns

The way my luck is running, if I was a politician I'd be honest.

–Rodney Dangerfield

I'd rather wake up in the middle of nowhere than in any city on Earth.

–Steve McQueen

The person who knows how to laugh at himself will never cease to be amused.

–Shirley Maclaine

A man properly must pay the fiddler. In my case it so happened that a whole symphony orchestra had to be subsidized.

–John Barrymore

Music is my mistress, and she plays second fiddle to no one.

–Louis Armstrong

I wrote a song about dental floss, but did anyone's teeth get cleaner?

–Frank Zappa

Outside of a dog, a book is a man's best friend. Inside a dog, it's too dark to read.

–Groucho Marx

A movie is like a salmon headed upstream. There are a lot of things that are trying to keep it from getting there. That's not to say that I'm infallible, I'm the one that knows best, but somebody has to have a point of view and stand up for it.

−**Kevin Costner**

I was once thrown out of a mental hospital for depressing the other patients.

−**Oscar Levant**

I have bursts of being a lady, but it doesn't last long.

−**Shelly Winters**

There are three things I've yet to do: Opera, rodeo and porno.

−**Bea Arthur**

Rawhide was great fun at first...But after seven years of playing the same character in the same wardrobe you get kind of edgy...when you find yourself putting lip gloss on your horse you know you're becoming ill.

−**Clint Eastwood**

I find television very educating. Every time somebody turns on the set, I go into the other room and read a book.

−**Groucho Marx**

Television has brought back murder into the home—where it belongs.

−**Alfred Hitchcock**

In California they don't throw their garbage away—they make it into television shows.
— **Woody Allen in** *Annie Hall*

Work is the only reason I leave home. I'm not a tourist. I don't travel for pleasure. I don't take vacations. I only leave the house when I have something to do.
— **Frank Zappa**

Reality is something you rise above.
— **Liza Minnelli**

I used to feel a little guilty about owning two planes. Then, one day, I had a long talk with myself. I said "Hell, John, you're allowed to change with your success. Your fans want you to change." So instead of a house I bought an airplane.
— **John Travolta**

I'm everything you were afraid your little girl would grow up to be—and your little boy.
— **Bette Midler**

It's better to be quotable than honest.
— **Tom Stoppard**

The good die young—because they see it's no use living if you've got to be good.
— **John Barrymore**

An actor is supposed to be a sensitive instrument. Isaac Stern takes good care of his violin. What if everybody jumped on his violin?

–**Marilyn Monroe**

Luck is a matter of preparation meeting opportunity.

–**Oprah Winfrey**

Cocaine is God's way of saying you're making too much money.

–**Robin Williams**

I'm old. I'm young. I'm intelligent. I'm stupid.

–**Warren Beatty**

You can take all of the sincerity in Hollywood and put into a mosquito's navel and still have room for two caraway seeds and a producer's heart.

–**Fred Allen**

Miami Beach is where neon goes to die.

–**Lenny Bruce**

Rock 'n' roll is a bit like Las Vegas: guys get dressed up in their sisters' clothes pretending to be angry, but not really angry about anything.

–**Sting**

The biggest misconception people have about me is that I'm stupid.

–**Billy Idol**

If I wasn't doing this, I'd probably be a depressed little person.

—**Britney Spears**

I'm a meathead. I can't help it, man. You've got smart people and you've got dumb people.

—**Keanu Reeves**

I'm very driven, even though I don't drive.

—**Debbie Gibson**

When I'm singing a ballad and a pair of underwear lands on my head, I hate that. It really kills the mood.

—**Tom Jones**

If Presidents don't do it to their wives, they do it to their country.

—**Mel Brooks**

I always throw my golf club in the direction I'm going.

—**Ronald Reagan**

I don't feel we did wrong in taking this great country away from them. There were great numbers of people who needed new land, and the Indians were selfishly trying to keep it for themselves.

—**John Wayne**

I wanted to perform, I wanted to write songs, and I wanted to get lots of chicks.

—**James Taylor on why he got into music**

Before I got into rock 'n' roll, I was going to be a dentist.

−Greg Allman

How would you define jazz? Man, if you gotta ask, you'll never know.

−Louis Armstrong

What do you call a Spice Girl with two brain cells? .... pregnant.

−Mel C. a.k.a. Sporty Spice

Boy, those French! They have a different word for everything.

−Steve Martin

I don't mind if the Japanese buy the Mariners, just as long as they don't let Yoko Ono sing the national anthem at their games.

−Jay Leno

When people asked me what I did for a living, I told them, "I do pilots." They all thought I was a stewardess.

−Suzanne Somers

There are two dilemmas that rattle the human skull: How do you hang on to someone who won't stay? And how do you get rid of someone who won't go?

−Danny Devito in *The War of the Roses*

I don't think anyone should write his autobiography until after he's dead.

−Samuel Goldwyn

France is a country where the money falls apart and you can't tear the toilet paper.

– Billy Wilder

America is the country where you buy a lifetime supply of aspirin for one dollar and use it up in two weeks.

– John Barrymore

If it weren't for Abe [Lincoln], I'd still be on the open market.

– Dick Gregory

I will clean house when Sears comes out with a riding vacuum cleaner.

– Roseanne Barr

Happiness is seeing the muscular lifeguard all the girls were admiring leave the beach hand in hand with another muscular lifeguard.

– Johnny Carson

If you think it's hard to meet new people, try picking up the wrong golf ball.

– Jack Lemmon

I'd move to Los Angeles if New Zealand and Australia were swallowed up by a tidal wave, if there was bubonic plague in England and if the continent of Africa disappeared from some Martian attack.

– Russell Crowe

I'm the original take-orders girl.

−Judy Garland

I can't get no respect.

−Rodney Dangerfield

I personally think we developed language because of our deep need to complain.

−Lily Tomlin

I love my name. I think it's great. I mean Schwarzenegger− what's that? How are you going to complain about Zellweger?

−Renee Zellweger

The number-one fear in life is public speaking, and the number-two fear is death. This means that if you go to a funeral, you're better off in the casket than giving the eulogy.

−Jerry Seinfeld

Man is the only animal that can be skinned more than once.

−Jimmy Durante

I sing from the heart... I sing the words of a song and really feel them, from the top of my head to the tip of my toes... I sing as though my life depends on it, and if I ever stop doing that then I'll stop living.

−Mario Lanza

Fisbeetarianism is the belief that when you die, your soul goes up on the roof and gets stuck.

−George Carlin

You know it's going to hell when the best rapper out there is white and the best golfer is black.

–Charles Barkley

I like talking. I like acting. Running and jumping and ducking bullets is not my idea of a good day.

–Denzel Washington

If God wanted us to fly, He would have given us tickets.

–Mel Brooks

Golf: On one hole I'm like Arnold Palmer, and on the next like Lilli Palmer.

–Sean Connery

If it's a woman, it's caustic; if it's a man, it's authoritative.

–Barbara Walters

Egotism: usually just a case of mistaken nonentity.

–Barbara Stanwyk

Somebody has to do something, and it's just incredibly pathetic that it has to be us.

–Jerry Garcia

If it weren't for Philo T. Farnsworth inventor of television, we'd still be eating frozen radio dinners.

–Johnny Carson

My mobster days are over.

–James Gandolfini

After *The Wizard of Oz*, I was typecast as a lion, and there aren't that many parts for lions.
—**Bert Lahr**

In the fight between you and the world, back the world.
—**Frank Zappa**

I wish to be cremated. One tenth of my ashes shall be given to my agent, as written in our contract.
—**Groucho Marx**

I'd rather be dead than singing "Satisfaction" when I'm forty-five.
—**Mick Jagger**